Marleen Gorris

Marleen Gorris

Practices of Resistance

Sue Thornham

EDINBURGH
University Press

Edinburgh University Press is one of the leading university presses in the UK. We publish academic books and journals in our selected subject areas across the humanities and social sciences, combining cutting-edge scholarship with high editorial and production values to produce academic works of lasting importance. For more information visit our website: edinburghuniversitypress.com

We are committed to making research available to a wide audience and are pleased to be publishing Platinum Open Access ebook editions of titles in this series.

Grateful acknowledgement is made to the sources listed in the List of Illustrations for permission to reproduce material previously published elsewhere. Every effort has been made to trace the copyright holders, but if any have been inadvertently overlooked, the publisher will be pleased to make the necessary arrangements at the first opportunity.

Edinburgh University Press Ltd
13 Infirmary Street
Edinburgh EH1 1LT

Typeset in 12/14 Arno and Myriad by
IDSUK (DataConnection) Ltd

A CIP record for this book is available from the British Library

ISBN 978 1 3995 2796 5 (hardback)
ISBN 978 1 3995 2797 2 (paperback)
ISBN 978 1 3995 2798 9 (webready PDF)
ISBN 978 1 3995 2799 6 (epub)

Contents

Figures

Acknowledgments

I should like to thank Ali Ramsey, who first suggested that I write this book. Most of all, I'd like to thank Marleen Gorris, who responded to my queries with such patience and generosity.

Introduction: resistance, time and women's filmmaking

Marleen Gorris is a filmmaker known chiefly for two films: *A Question of Silence* (1982), her fiercely, triumphally feminist first film, in which three 'very ordinary' women come together by chance in a women's clothing boutique and ritually murder its male owner; and *Antonia's Line* (1995), her fourth film and winner of the 1996 Oscar for Best Foreign Language Film, which traces four generations of Antonia's female 'line' in the matriarchal community she establishes in post-war rural Holland. Both of these films have been extensively discussed, though rarely together, and appear widely on university syllabuses. Her second Dutch language film, *Broken Mirrors* (1984), and her five films in English, however, have received far less, and in some cases no critical attention. In this book I shall consider Gorris's films, which stretch over a period of nearly thirty years, in relation to a number of feminist theoretical ideas: ideas centred on questions of vulnerability, resistance and a relationally constituted self, and on the challenges these ideas pose to conventional understandings of time and space.

My title, 'Practices of Resistance' is in part a nod to the origins of Gorris's filmmaking in the radical feminist politics of the late 1970s and early 1980s, when the term became central to both political activism and cultural theory. Volumes like *Fight Back! Feminist Resistance to Male Violence* of 1981, an anthology and resource book 'for all of us who struggle with [male] violence in our lives' (Delacoste and Newman 1981),[1] in which both self-defence and survival feature as modes of resistance, found their more theoretical counterparts in volumes such as *Resistance through Rituals* (Hall and Jefferson 1976), the volume on youth sub-cultures from the Birmingham Centre for Contemporary Cultural Studies, where Angela McRobbie and Jenny Garber adapted the Centre's Gramscian approach to the analysis of girls' strategies of resistance to their 'sexual subordination' (1976: 221). A little later, Michel Foucault's disciplinary model of power in which power relations are always unstable and subject to resistance was similarly appropriated by feminist theorists analysing forms of gendered oppression and women's resistance to it.[2] In her 'Lessons from Foucault and Feminism', for example, Karen Faith defines feminism *as* resistance. 'Feminism, as I know it,' she writes, 'is resistance to invisibility and silencing. It is the recognition that resistance to gendered power relations is both integral to and distinct from all other resistances to global injustice.' It is 'both a spontaneous reaction against and a strategic resistance to existing power relations' (1994: 37, 47).

Resistance, then, is a term that has been frequently employed in academic discussions of *A Question of Silence*, which has been seen both as portraying women's resistance to patriarchal violence (Smelik 1998: 91) and as resisting conventional cinematic constructions of femininity (Nikolopoulou 2011: 8). More recently however, as Kristyn Gorton (2021) has pointed out, the idea of feminist resistance has become less visible in both academic and media discourse than its more individualist counterpart: women's 'resilience'. Whilst both terms are, as Sarah Bracke (2016: 69) has argued, tied to ideas of vulnerability, resistance carries the sense of active opposition, of 'actions involving consciousness, collective action, and direct challenges to structures of power' (Rubin, 1996: 245). By contrast, the resilient woman is, writes Bracke, she 'who continues to survive patriarchy . . . and is considered individually responsible for her survival' (2016: 65). If resistance implies defying or actively contesting vulnerability, resilience is 'conceptually designed' to overcome it – 'to contain and evade it, to bounce back from it, to minimize its traces' (ibid.: 69). For cultural theorists like

Bracke, Rosalind Gill (Gill and Orgad, 2017, 2018) and Angela McRobbie (2020), it is an aspect of 'gendered neoliberalism', in which women are 'hailed as emblematic "bounce-backable" subjects' (Gill and Orgad 2018: 477), so that the post-feminist heroine of popular culture can be hailed as the ultimate resilient subject.

Resistance, and its relationship to vulnerability, have also been subject to theoretical revision, however. Reimagined not as the opposite of resistance but as 'part of the very meaning or action of resistance itself' (Butler et al.: 2016: 1), vulnerability has been linked to the feminist idea of a relationally constituted self (Butler 2004a, Butler et al. 2016), and to the rethinking of time and space that such an idea implies (Baraitser 2017, Baraitser and Riley 2016). It is a move we can see foreshadowed in Linda Williams' 1988 essay on Gorris's first film, where her exploration of the nature of the resistance offered in the film takes us into rather more complex territory than most early discussions of it. Drawing on Elaine Showalter's account of the strategies women have devised to 'resist the silence imposed upon them in public life' (1981: 192), she follows Showalter's argument that women's cultural productions operate within a 'wild zone' on the margins of, but not quite captured by, the boundaries of the dominant male culture. It is a zone that might be conceptualised in terms of space, as a place 'where women congregate' (Williams 1988: 109), in terms of shared experience – as a subordinate and vulnerable women's culture – or, suggests Showalter, more 'metaphysically', in terms of a consciousness tied to the imaginary and articulated only on the borders, or in the interstices, of dominant cultural expression (1981: 200). It is this shared zone, suggests Williams, that is imagined in Gorris's film, as a space–time in which both regulatory and cinematic language are disrupted, linear time is suspended, and unspoken, corporeal relationships between women are foregrounded. It is this relationship between vulnerability, both linguistic and corporeal, and an always politicised resistance, and the connection of both to a relational self and to expanded and/or disrupted notions of time, space and community, that I will explore in relation to Gorris's films. First, however, I want to further outline the theoretical arguments I shall be deploying.

Resistance, vulnerability and women's spaces

The idea that the human subject is relational and embodied, and characterised by a fundamental vulnerability, is not new; it has been proposed by feminist theorists from Nancy Chodorow (1978) onwards, as a counter to the concept of the sovereign, autonomous, rationalist subject central to ideas of linear history and progress. Vulnerability is, however, a 'sticky' concept (Honkasalo 2018), one that has both a complex history and a contested critical value, not least within feminist thought. The idea that this is a mode of subjectivity characteristic of women and implying an ethics of care, found, for example, in the work of Carol Gilligan (1982), can be seen as simply reinforcing women's subordinate status. It can seem to suggest, too, that women, like other disadvantaged groups, in being particularly vulnerable are particularly in need of protection from those who are *not* vulnerable. For these dominant groups it can imply the need to master, or at least disavow, a characteristic that is seen as both disempowering and othering. Yet if viewed as a shared *human* characteristic, it can seem to ignore very real structural power differences. If, however, we define it as a constitutive openness to others, 'part of our material and corporeal relations' (Cavarero with Bertolino 2008: 141–2), vulnerability can imply a radically different concept of the human subject, one grounded in relationality and always embodied.

It is in the work of Judith Butler that we find the most complex, and at times difficult, working through of the concept, and one that links it also to the idea of resistance. In *The Psychic Life of Power* (1997), her psychoanalytically inflected account of subject formation, she describes human subjects as 'constituted in primary vulnerability' (1997: 20). At this point, however, she defines this as a vulnerability to power – to social norms, including that of gender, that we internalise as 'psychic phenomena' (ibid.: 21). Living out these norms renders us at once socially intelligible – able to speak, act and be understood as subjects – and open to exploitation. The problem is then how to theorise political resistance, given that as subjects we are attached to the norms and structures that render us intelligible and our lives socially liveable. Butler's answer is that the need for constant reiteration of these norms, in the form of social practices, renders them susceptible to historical transformation, a transformation that is made possible because, whilst our agency as subjects is enabled by subjection to these norms, '[a]gency always exceeds the power by which it is enabled' (ibid.: 15).

The concern to conceptualise a politics of resistance even in circumstances in which our 'primary vulnerability' is to power, and agency itself is an effect of power, is central to *The Psychic Life of Power*. Psychic rather than corporeal, however, the vulnerability thus conceptualised seems remote from the radical openness to others described above. In Butler's later *Precarious Life* (2004a), however, we find a far more corporeal subject, whose vulnerability is described in phenomenological rather than psycho-social terms. Butler now describes vulnerability as 'a vulnerability to the other that is part of bodily life', a 'relationality that is composed neither exclusively of myself nor you, but is to be conceived as *the tie* by which those terms are differentiated and related' (2004a: 29, 22, original italics). This vulnerability is a matter of touch, memory, sensation, affect. In it, she argues, we might find 'a basis for community' that is both ethical and political (ibid.: 19–22). In her 2016 essay 'Rethinking Vulnerability and Resistance', this is developed further. Part of what a body is, she writes, 'is its dependency on other bodies and networks of support'; it is 'defined by the relations that make its own life and action possible' (2016: 16), and she explicitly opposes this understanding of the embodied subject to the 'masculinist ideal' of autonomy and mastery (ibid.: 24). In collective forms of resistance, she continues, this vulnerability can be mobilised, so that it becomes 'a way of being exposed and agentic at the same time'. Vulnerability is thus 'part of the very meaning of political resistance as an embodied enactment' (ibid.: 22).

This recent conceptualisation draws on the work of Adriana Cavarero, for whom it is our vulnerability to others that connects us, and the mutual recognition which follows that permits self-realisation or what Cavarero calls 'self-narration'. Women, who have been denied the space of such mutual exposure, she writes, have been denied self-realisation, speech and identity. Through the creation of women-only areas that are 'shared, contextual, and relational', however, they can generate spaces that are not only ones of 'reciprocal exhibition' and care but are also 'clearly perceived and affirmed as political' (Cavarero 2000: 59–60). Butler follows Cavarero in affirming a fundamental dependency on others that 'bind[s] us and out of which emerge our thinking and affiliation, the basis of our ... collective resistance' (2004a: 49). Crucially, however, she does not abandon her earlier insistence on another kind of vulnerability: that to the forms of institutional power that 'precede and condition our existence' (2016: 21). It is these operations of regulatory power, she writes, that produce the social norms which make us intelligible as subjects, and that therefore make possible the kind of mutual recognition that Cavarero advocates. Social and impersonal, however, and always preceding me and my desires, they also constrain and regulate what I can say and do.

Butler's formulation, then, tempers Cavarero's political optimism. Recognition and 'self-narration' cannot exist, she insists, outside 'a set of cultural norms and a field of power that condition us fundamentally'. We must therefore 'think through' the 'primary' embodied form of vulnerability proposed by both herself and Cavarero 'with a theory of power and recognition' (2004a: 45). The resulting account is complex and at times ambiguous, rendering vulnerability a double-edged concept at once entangled in social norms and a source of mutual recognition and resistance. It allows Butler, however, to account for the differential distribution of vulnerability – structural power differences mean that some groups are *more* exposed to exploitation and precarity. It also insists that we cannot conceptualise vulnerability as a source of community and resistance outside the power structures that both enable and constrain its mobilisation. The spaces of resistance envisaged by Cavarero can for Butler only exist in relation to dominant political and historical structures. To frame her argument slightly differently, the marginalised and feminised spaces and temporalities of relationality and vulnerability-as-resistance might be socially, spatially and temporally abjected[3] in relation to the dominant social and political order, but they are never *outside* that order and its history.

Suspended time

Conceptualising these spaces of resistance also implies a rethinking of time. It is Lisa Baraitser who most fully develops this argument. A move away from the idea of an autonomous, independent human subject towards a concept of subjectivity as always relational, founded on a dependency, or vulnerability, that 'fundamentally defines us' (Butler 2014: 33) implies also, argues Baraitser, a move away from the idea of time as linear progression. Rather than a unidirectional flow that extends evenly from past into future and through which the individual, autonomous subject moves, a time of relationality or care is, she writes, a 'suspended' or 'stuck' time. It is the 'temporal practice of staying alongside others'; 'waiting, staying, delaying, enduring, returning [are] the temporal forms that care takes' (Baraitser 2017: 14). It is, she adds, a time lived '*in the feminine*' (ibid.: 79, original italics).

This last definition evokes Julia Kristeva's now classic essay on the relation between feminist struggle and the concept of time, though Baraitser is careful to differentiate her own theorisation from Kristeva's more essentialist conception. Kristeva famously distinguishes between 'the time of linear history' – time as 'project, teleology, departure, progression and arrival' (Moi 1986: 187), a time which is fundamentally masculine – and a temporality characterised by 'repetition and eternity': 'women's time'. Unlike linear time, 'which passes', this 'women's time' is cyclical and static – 'monumental' – and linked to female, and specifically maternal, subjectivity (Kristeva [1979] 1986a: 189–92). Feminist struggle in Europe, argues Kristeva, has passed through three phases, described at times as generational, at times as historically co-existing. In the first, women sought entry into linear, historical time and 'the socio-political life of nations' (ibid.: 193). In the second phase, beginning in the West after May 1968, women rejected history, politics and the symbolic order in favour of an identity rooted in sexual difference and seen as 'plural, fluid . . . non-identical' (ibid.: 194), and have fantasised a 'counter-society . . . imagined as harmonious' (ibid.: 202, original italics).

So far, Kristeva's phases have recognisable parallels in other histories of feminism (Hemmings 2011).[4] Kristeva's third phase, however, has proved far more problematic for feminist theory. It is ambiguously described as both existent and still to come, and envisages the dissolution of *all* identities, and therefore of feminism, in a play of individual differences. This will come with acceptance and understanding of the internal splitting that results from the entry of each subject, whether male or female, into the socio-symbolic order. What is apparent, however, is that the socio-symbolic order does not itself change in Kristeva's third, transcendent phase. The 'common destiny of the two sexes' (Kristeva [1979] 1986a: 198), it retains its phallocentric structure, whilst *women's* internal divisions arise specifically from their experience of maternity, which positions them at 'the threshold between nature and culture' (Kristeva [1977] 1986b: 297). Whether characterised as cyclicality, the timeless maternal or transcendence, for Kristeva women and 'women's time', it would seem, (will) remain outside linear time and history.

What might it take to re-think Kristeva's 'post-political' concept of 'women's time' in terms which *are* political – as, in Carol Watts' words (1998: 14), a temporality that interpellates women, in conditions that are not of their choosing, but might at the same time be imagined as a 'point of resistance to the rationalizations of capitalist modernity'? This is a question explored in Barbara Adam's authoritative study of time, *Timewatch* (1995). The opposition presented by Kristeva, between 'the time of linear history' and 'other', 'women's time', is one, argues Adam, that underpins much anthropological, historical and sociological thinking. 'Our Western time', she writes, is conceptualised as historical, linear, irreversible, changing, clock and calendar-based, decontextualised and abstract; the time of 'others' is in contrast cyclical, reversible, static, task and nature-based, and embedded. Western time is seen as neutral, objective; we live *in* time, as individual, autonomous subjects. This is, argues Adam, a very specific construction of time, one that serves the economics and ideologies of Western industrial societies, but its hegemony has the effect of rendering invisible, or actively repressing, forms of temporality incompatible with this dominant idea. These other forms of temporality include time that is process- or task-oriented, time that is generative and relational (*giving* time), time that is embedded and embodied, time of waiting or repetition: forms of time, in Baraitser's words, that are lived '*in the feminine*'. The hegemony of the dominant idea of time means, however, that we understand, and evaluate, the complexity of these other temporal experiences through its 'mediating filter' (Adam 1995: 99). Some forms of time, and some people's time, writes Adam, become 'shadow' time. Put differently, we might say that just as Anne McClintock (1995: 72) argues that some spaces (the prison, the brothel, the ghetto, the asylum) become 'abject zones', the repudiated yet constitutive spaces on which modernity and progress have depended but which they both disavow and police, so some forms of temporality become 'abject time'.

Adam is critical of the kind of essentialising of women's time as cyclical and/or process- and task-oriented found in Kristeva's essay. If such forms of temporality are most often time lived 'in the feminine', she writes, this is the outcome of structural and discursive power, not the result of women's greater closeness to nature. For Adam, there 'is no single time, only a multitude of times which interpenetrate and permeate our daily lives' (1995: 12).

Time is linear *and* cyclical; it is a matter of sequences, 'irreversible changes, records and identity' (ibid.: 15), but also of simultaneity: 'of mundane, extraordinary and global events, of past, present and future'. We are temporally extended in both time and space, so that our 'temporal being expands beyond our personal boundaries to significant others and even to strangers' (ibid.: 14–15). In similar fashion, Baraitser's focus on time as relational not linear, a kind of 'stopped' time that is nevertheless generative (2009: 79–80), sees it not as the essentialised or abject other to the time of history and progress but as both integral to historical time and, as its interruption or suspension, the temporal dimension of care, of 'affective, political and physical relationships' (2017: 53), and of possibility. These are experiences of time that have to do with states of dependency and vulnerability, but also with a relationship to 'histories of oppression and resistance, and histories of power and agency' (ibid.). They are connected to 'a history of feminist thought and practice that has always been concerned with lives "on hold"' (ibid.: 52).

'Maybe only the cinema could show it'

In a conversation with Baraitser published in 2016, Denise Riley discusses *Time Lived, Without its Flow,* Riley's account of her experience of time following the death of her adult son. Like Baraitser, she is concerned there with an experience of time *not* passing, but she is also concerned with the way in which this affects narrative. 'Once there's no longer any element of sequence, because that usual intuition of flowing time has been halted,' she writes in *Time Lived ...,* 'narration itself can't proceed .... Your very condition militates against narrative'. But she adds, 'Maybe only the cinema could show it' ([2012] 2020: 108).

In *Timewatch,* Adam identifies the emergence of the dominant Western linear perspective with two representational modes. The first is visual: the development of painting's 'linear-perspective vision of reality', in which the spectator is positioned outside the scene portrayed and the scene itself arranged as a unified whole for that spectator. The illusion is of a spatial medium that is neutral, homogeneous and infinite. Its implied spectator, separated from the world that unfolds before his controlling viewpoint, is abstract, disembodied and powerful, the autonomous Western subject 'capable of being everywhere at once and nowhere in particular' (Adam 1995: 152; quoting Ingold 1993: 155). The second representational mode is temporal. Here Adam draws on the work of Elizabeth Deeds Ermarth to identify the perspective of Western 'clock time' with realist narrative. This too, she argues, is centred on an implied consciousness 'capable of being everywhere at once and nowhere in particular', achieved in this case through the 'narrator as nobody' (Adam 1995: 152; Ermarth 1998: 65–92), positioned outside the narrative and organising its temporal field. Like Adam, Ermarth identifies the temporal counterpart of the visual system of single-point perspective as 'history', and she too writes of 'women's history' as fragmented, interrupted, a time of waiting and 'temporal arrest' (1989: 42). She is more concerned, however, to explore how fictional narratives work to construct time as 'history': as neutrality, order and progress.

Just as the constructed viewpoint in painting organises the visual field and positions the spectator as autonomous and unified subject, writes Ermarth, so the narrative perspective in realist fiction 'unifies time and rationalizes consciousness' (1998: 25). The multiple temporalities of characters, relationships, consciousnesses and events are organised into a single linear structure within which individual temporalities are hierarchically organised. Since in realist fiction each 'momentary present' is already past, it is given its significance within a pattern that both understands time as a linear progression of events and *constructs* it as such. Our stories construct our notion of time and with it reinforce the worldview of which it is an expression. Fragmented times 'become a single time', and 'multiplicity, variety, disparity, ambiguity' are absorbed into a single temporal sequence (ibid: 46–7) that confirms the linear continuity of time, the rational progression of past, present and future, and the rightness of the underlying conceptual framework that gives meaning to this structure. The narrative structure of realist fiction, writes Ermarth, 'coordinates present and present, past and past, so that the various points of view all belong to a single temporal continuity that approaches clock time' (ibid.: 80). The consciousness that it implies transcends particulars; it is rational, abstract and possessed of a knowledge (of the 'hidden order' of things) that confers control (ibid.: 58, 64). Finally, the central character who moves through this temporal structure is active and mobile. It is their mobility that reveals this hidden order. 'Stasis' – Baraitser's 'suspended time' – is identified with ontological and moral failure (ibid.: 56).

Cinema of course, as Laura Mulvey famously writes, contains both of Ermarth's representational modes, 'controlling [both] the dimension of time (editing, narrative) and . . . the dimension of space (changes in distance, editing)' (Mulvey [1975] 2009: 25). Its narrating agent, the camera, is famously 'capable of being everywhere at once and nowhere in particular'. For Mulvey, as for Ermarth, it is the way in which these cinematic codes reinforce 'formative external structures' (ibid.) that renders mainstream cinema so problematic, but other theorists have also emphasised the potential for disruption in cinema's complex temporal structure. Like Adam, Mary Ann Doane writes of the way in which narrative, which quickly became cinema's primary mode, structures time and makes it legible, working 'to familiarize temporal irreversibility, in its unrelenting forward movement' (2002: 27). A crucial agent in modernity's construction of time, cinema is nevertheless unreliable, she writes: its capacity to show as well as record, to represent duration as well as linear progress, to 'coagulat[e]' (ibid.: 170) as well as linearise time rendering it always potentially 'unstable' (ibid.: 169). For narrative theorists like Seymour Chatman this makes it an inferior medium, unable to render interiority and caught up in the spatiality it depicts, its 'plenitude of visual details' constituting an 'excessive particularity' (1981: 122). For Chatman, cinema is always threatened by a kind of material or corporeal excess which is also an emptiness of meaning, to be rescued only by the relentless 'force of plot' (ibid.: 126) which pushes its static visuality into motion and linear temporality. For Riley, as we see in the quotation that heads this section, it offers the possibility of representing the kind of suspended, relational time that narrative linearity represses.

Gendering machines

For both Mulvey and Doane the organisation of cinematic syntax to privilege narrative linearity is also the organisation of sexual difference to privilege the masculine subject and hetero-sexuality. This is an identification always implicit in the work of narrative theorists like Chatman or Gérard Genette (1982), for whom description – static, beautiful, seductive – must always be mastered by narration's active, mobile masculinity, but it becomes most explicit in work on genre. The argument that popular genres not only function as regulatory systems for mainstream narrative texts (Neale 1980: 20), but also perform 'social and cultural functions' (ibid.: 45), including that of 'the construction and maintenance of sexual identity and difference' (ibid.: 56), was one developed by many theorists in the 1980s (Fiske 1987, Curti 1988, Tulloch 1990). For John Fiske, for example, 'masculine' genres emphasise 'freedom, individualism, leadership and power'; their protagonists operate in the public domain and their narratives concentrate on action, compress time and push towards narrative resolution (1987: 2014–21). Less valued 'feminine' genres, in contrast, focus on community and relationships; they emphasise the domestic and expand time, deferring narrative closure (ibid.: 2015–20).

Understanding the gendering of popular genres, then, becomes a way of connecting a theory of social and cultural power with a theory of the operations of cultural texts. This is most clearly articulated in the work of Lauren Berlant. Like Judith Butler (2004b: 41), Berlant sees gender as a 'norm [that] governs the social intelligibility of action',[5] but her understanding of how this works centres on narrative. 'Berlant', writes Virginia Jackson, 'is really a genre theorist' (2015), but for her, genre as discursive or aesthetic category 'becomes indistinguishable from genre as a shaping force in lived experience'. A genre for Berlant becomes 'a loose affectively-invested zone of expectations about the narrative shape a situation will take' (2011b: 2), a definition which takes in both lived and fictional practices. Relationality, or intimacy, for example, 'involves an aspiration for a narrative about something shared, a story about both oneself and others that will turn out in a particular way' (1998: 281). When like other feminist theorists she looks at the ideological, aesthetic and temporal structures of 'women's genres', then, the circularity and temporal non-progression identified by writers like Mary Ann Doane (1987) and Tania Modleski (1987) becomes a characteristic not only of the fictional texts she examines but of the construction of femininity itself. It is this which is circular: 'a perfect form, a sphere infused with activities of ongoing attachment that can at the same time look and feel like a zero' (Berlant 2008: 20). The texts of popular culture, she writes, function as 'gendering machines' (ibid.: 35), organising our affects and experiences according to hegemonic generic conventions. They structure not just our modes of living but our fantasies of what is normal and what might be possible, and Berlant is concerned, in her own interpretive narrative, to trace both these organising stories and our affective investments in their normative fantasies.

Berlant is critical of Butler's turn to the idea of vulnerability as a primary embodied openness generative of relationality. For her it bypasses too easily the power of our attachments to normative authority, the ways in which these structure relationality, and the role of fantasy and the unconscious in sustaining our attachments. Instead, she works critically with these attachments and the narratives they engender, attending both to their generic normativity and to the interruptions or 'glitches' in them (2011a: 198). But like Butler, it is to 'bodies moving in space performing affectively laden gestures' that she looks for these interruptions, and for 'new potential conditions of solidarity' (ibid.: 201). In this, her case studies may be both cinematic narratives and modes of lived experience. For her, cinema functions as generic shaper of the fantasies which structure our everyday lives, but it may also act as investigator of their consequences and of the possibilities generated by their interruption. These interruptions register as temporal and narrative disruptions, moments of 'impasse' which are 'spaces of time lived without a narrative genre', where norms of 'self-intelligibility' are threatened by 'embodied perturbation[s]', and we watch 'subjects getting, losing, and keeping their bearing within a thick present' (ibid.: 198–9). For Berlant, then, cinema is a powerful force both culturally and politically. Its genres structure our fantasies, affective life and sense of what is possible, and mask inequalities and exploitation, but they are also open to disruption and perhaps resignification.

Resistance, time and the filmmaking of Marleen Gorris

Uniting the ideas explored above are questions of time, genre and resistance. Berlant's impasse, which is 'a middle without boundaries, edges, a shape' (2011a: 200), is also Baraitser's 'suspended' time (Baraitser 2017: 51). Both contest the singular conception of time as linear, unidirectional flow, and insist that attention be paid to the multiplicity, simultaneity and permeability of lived temporalities, and to the ways in which time may be suspended, layered and extended. Suspended time can also be relational time, and to consider this is also to consider the gendered nature of these temporal modes, and the ways in which this gendering might be theorised, politicised and disrupted. It is also to think about narrative, for if a lived but suspended time is antithetical to narrative, as Riley writes in *Time Lived*, then we need to consider the functioning of narrative, and its dominant genres, in constructing our temporal imaginaries (2020: 108). Can a filmmaking practice which deploys but interrupts and disturbs the conventions of a range of cinematic genres *show*, in the way Riley suggests, both our attachment to these stories as normative fantasies and the ways in which they might be resisted and disrupted through other, perhaps abjected, temporalities and modes of living in and with time?

The cinema of Marleen Gorris, I argue, constitutes one such practice. Her films, she insisted, are realist, employing conventional narrative forms and genres (Smelik 1990: 247), but they are also persistently concerned to imagine the possibility of a relationally constituted community of women, and some men, whose subjects are marked by vulnerability (corporeal, economic, political) but are resistant and agentic. How, they ask, might we imagine such a space within, or in relation to, the historical world as we know it, and to social, narrative and generic structures which position the female subject in very specific ways? The spaces she imagines may exist alongside or within, in the interstices or on the margins of, the historical world and the genres through which it has been imagined. Within them, time may be expanded or slowed, with temporal impossibilities, repetition and doubling, and genre and its underpinning assumptions played with or radically disrupted.

Gorris' most celebrated film is *Antonia's Line* (1995), the film which presents the most fully articulated vision of the female-centred community she envisions and of its re-imagined relationship to both space and time. The film is unusual in Gorris's oeuvre, however, in the relative lightness of its play with cinematic genre. Elsewhere, in both her early Dutch-language and her later English-language films, where she directed from the scripts of others, genre is employed as a determining structure within and against which Gorris works, playing with and disrupting its conventions. Her first two films concern gendered violence and its representation, and employ the conventions of the detective film, the courtroom drama and the serial killer narrative. In thinking of them as radical feminist cinema, it is easy to forget the context of their making, a moment when the dominant cinema of America, as Sarah Hagelin has argued, 'seemed obsessed with masculine white men', producing films in which violence is repeatedly inflicted on the female body and traditional notions of masculinity reasserted (2013: 13–14). The *Death Wish, Rocky* and *Rambo* franchises all saw high-grossing releases in 1982, the year in which *A Question of Silence* was released, and the fourth Dirty Harry film, *Sudden Impact,* a year later. The *Die Hard* and *Lethal Weapon* franchises were to begin in the next few years.

In contrast, Gorris' films at the end of the 1990s, *Mrs Dalloway* (1997) and *The Luzhin Defence* (2000), are adaptations and costume dramas, but here, too, I want to argue that she plays with and against generic conventions which had by then become well established, as well as with the conventions of a literary past (Vidal 2005). *Carolina,* which followed in 2003, similarly plays with and, more interestingly, against the conventions of romantic comedy. Her final film, *Within the Whirlwind* (2009), is another adaptation, based on a two-volume memoir by Eugenia Ginzburg, a Communist Party member and university professor who was arrested, tried and sentenced during Stalin's purges of the 1930s and then spent eighteen years in prisons and Siberian labour camps. Delivered, according to its star, Emily Watson, 'pretty much the day the market crashed' (Rees 2011), it was not distributed and has barely been reviewed. Here Gorris plays with and against the conventions of both the memoir and the historical epic.

Finally then, this moment – when Gorris has made her final film (a film about Dr James Miranda Barry was scheduled for 2012 but never made, and in 2017 she announced her retirement from filmmaking), and her first three films, so long unavailable, can now be bought in restored versions – seems an appropriate one at which to consider her films as a whole.

Notes

1 The publisher's description reads:

> *Fight Back! Feminist Resistance to Male Violence* is a resource for all of us who struggle with violence in our lives. In it are stories of personal survival, articles on the shelter and rape crisis movements, strategies for defending women who kill their attackers, survival tactics, documentation of law-challenging

actions women have taken against pornography, rape, battering and sexual harassment across the country. Fight Back! includes a comprehensive directory of rape crisis centers, shelters for battered women, support services for incest victims, legal resources, karate and self-defense schools and instructors, newsletters, political and resource organizations.

2 See for example Diamond and Quinby (eds.) (1988), McNay (1992), Radtke and Stam (eds.) (1995).

3 Anu Koivunen, Katariina Kyrölä and Ingrid Ryberg (2018: 7) see the concept of abjection as 'intimately tied to' vulnerability, since both can be understood as 'a tension between subjugation and resistance, embedded both in societal and psychic structures', and both 'are keenly connected to affect and embodiment'. Abjection, however, 'implies disgust, shame, and fear to a wholly different degree than vulnerability' (Ibid.: 7–8).

4 She is, however, overtly hostile to the imagined societies of the second phase, which she identifies with a destructiveness that is the result of 'a paranoid counter-investment' in existing power structures (Kristeva 1986a: 201).

5 She argues in very similar terms that the overlapping categories of genre and gender are 'the two clarifying institutions of social intelligibility' (Berlant 2011a: 176).

1

Time and the politics of resistance

Reflecting on Julia Kristeva's idea of 'women's time', Elizabeth Deeds Ermarth (1989: 37) writes that in terms of conventional definitions of time – what Kristeva calls 'linear time . . . the time of project and history' ([1979] 1986a: 193) – the concept is meaningless. The discourse of historical time, argues Ermarth, depends on the exclusion or repression of women, so that 'so long as time means what our novelistic and social conventions have told us it means', the idea of 'women's time' is impossible. For Ermarth, as we have seen (see pp. 11–12), this temporal discourse organises not only 'history' but also the narratives of realist fiction. Within it, she argues, women's otherness, and opposition, to the dominant concept of time are rewritten as a story of necessary sacrifice: necessary in order that the social order might be reaffirmed. She adds that this endlessly repeated 'sacrificial plot' is one particularly familiar to us from the detective genre, 'where the police or problem solvers are usually men and the victims usually women for whom the threat of rape or death is the logical outcome of their magnified vulnerability; he is the power that unfolds truth while she is the (justified) sacrifice' (1989: 37, 41).

In the writing by women that she examines, in contrast, Ermarth finds that, absent as subjects from the discourse of history, theirs is a language of 'solitude and anguish', the experience they recount one of 'temporal arrest'. Excluded from history, the women of these texts 'inhabit a situation . . . of fragmentation and paralysis that contrasts utterly with the medium of action and event' (ibid.: 42–3). She concludes that if women are to be able to articulate their lives 'as discourse and not Other', what is needed is an uncovering of 'new modes of liveable time' and an 'unsettling' of 'meaning and subject', 'throwing the emphasis off what is finished, conclusive, static, identified and on to what is open, playful, mobile, relational' (ibid.: 43, 45).

Ermarth's essay was published in 1989 and written in the mid-1980s. In 1982 Marleen Gorris's first film, *De Stilte Rond Christine M*, was released, and distributed in the UK and US as *A Question of Silence*.[1] Its subject is precisely the 'sacrificial plot' that Ermarth describes, its method the deployment, disruption and rewriting of the investigative narrative that she outlines. Through this radical disruption it traces a female journey from the isolation, fragmentation and temporal arrest of Ermarth's account, to the possibility of self-articulation through community. Its '(justified) sacrifice' is not a vulnerable woman, but a man. The result, in Ermarth's terms, is an unsettling of meaning and subject in a process that is both radically disturbing and 'open, playful, mobile, relational'.

A Question of Silence (*De Stilte Rond Christine M*) (1982)

A Question of Silence's investigative narrative follows court-appointed psychiatrist Janine van den Bos (Cox Habbema), whose task is to determine, through a series of interviews, whether three 'very ordinary'[2] and unconnected women – Christine (Edda Barends), a young housewife and mother, An (Nellie Frijda), a café worker, and Andrea (Henriëtte Tol), a secretary – can be held accountable for their seemingly random and gratuitous murder of a male boutique owner (Dolf de Vries). Through flashbacks we see the lives of the women, and then the murder itself. The final twenty minutes depict the trial, in which Janine, in the face of repeated appeals to the professional 'objectivity' to be expected 'even from a woman', unexpectedly pronounces the women sane, despite the absence of a personal motive. In response, the prosecuting counsel (Erik Plooyer) insists – perfectly accurately in legal terms – that he can 'see no difference between this case and, let's say . . . if three men had killed the female owner of a shop'. The ensuing female laughter – a laughter reproduced, according to B. Ruby Rich ([1984] 1998: 324), Barbara Kruger (1983: 83) and Anneke Smelik (2023: 3), by the women in the film's first cinema audiences – results in the removal of the three women, still laughing, with the trial to continue in their absence. Janine, also laughing, exits the court.

Winner of the 1982 Golden Calf award for best feature film at the Netherlands Film Festival, and of the Grand Prix at the Créteil International Women's Film Festival, the film met with an extraordinarily divided critical reception, as a number of feminist critics detailed in essays of the 1980s.[3] Whilst feminist reviewers praised the film's generic subversions, technical complexity, humour and intelligent radicalism,[4] other, largely male reviewers insisted that its 'shrillness' (*Sunday Telegraph*), 'absurd[. . .] overstat[ement]' (*Daily Mail*), 'lack[of] any wit or sparkle' (*Morning Star*), 'inconsistency and unpredictability' and 'lumbering and unintelligent dialogue' (*The Scotsman*) all meant that, in the words of Janet Maslin of the *New York Times*, 'the feminist cause will not be well served by *A Question of Silence*'.[5] A number of these reviewers were careful to insist on the rationality of their own stance – 'I speak without bias . . .' (*New Musical Express*); 'No-one is more sympathetic than I to the reasoned arguments of women's rights campaigners . . .' (*Daily Mail*). It was Philip French in the *Observer* and Milton Shulman of the *Standard*, however, who most forcibly articulated their position.

For French, whose review exudes contempt for both the film and its presumed audience of 'young people of average intelligence or less', *A Question of Silence* was 'intrinsically stupid', 'reckless' and 'rigid': 'as rigid in its thinking as any hard-line Stalinist movie' (1983: 30). Shulman goes even further in identifying his own position with 'reason', which he explains is 'man's reason', and the film with its 'senseless' rejection by the women's movement in its 'hatred of men'. The film's 'argument', he continues, 'would have justified the Nazis exterminating Jews, Herod's slaughter of babies and the lynching of blacks'. '[C]ompared to the logic of this film's message', he continues – which is to justify women's murder of men 'purely on the grounds of . . . sex' – genocide 'is a comparatively modest moral device'. He ends with a warning to these disruptive women: like the women who 'marched against the Shah' in pre-revolutionary Iran, they may find themselves discovering what real oppression is (1983: 23).

What is clear, I hope, from my brief summary of the film, is that Shulman's stance exactly reproduces that of Gorris's courtroom. Like the film's prosecuting counsel, French and Shulman identify their own position with objectivity, reason and intelligence, and its subversion or rejection with a dangerous and 'senseless' irrationality. Like him, they can see no difference between (the film's representation of) a single act of murder committed by women who are excluded from the structures of social and discursive power and the brutal exercise of systemic, oppressive power found in genocide and mass slaughter – though Shulman's final warning suggests that, at some level at least, he is well aware of where power lies. For feminist critics, however, the film was above all both about and in itself a form of resistance. For Anneke Smelik, 'the murder is an act of resistance' (1993: 352), for Linda Dittmar (1986: 80) the film explores 'strategies of feminist solidarity and resistance', for Jeanette Murphy it 'leads us towards a possible form of resistance – separatism' (1986: 101), whilst for Linda Williams (1988: 114) its power 'lies in its resistance of all the male paradigms through which female deviance has been understood'. Less written about over the past twenty years, and unavailable on DVD until 2023, the film has nevertheless retained its provocative resonance. In an essay of 2022, Amelia Groom points out that, as well as praise, it continues to attract 'confused vitriol' in user reviews on IMDB, whilst in contrast Mark Kermode's 2023 review of *Women Talking*, Sarah Polley's film about women's silencing and the power of their collective speech, references as a comparison 'Marleen Gorris's electrifying

1982 feminist psychodrama *A Question of Silence*, reviewed almost exactly forty years earlier.

What, then, provoked these early responses? The film, as critics have pointed out (Johnston 1983, Ramanathan 1992), is structured as a detective narrative: with the double plot structure typical of the genre, in which we follow the investigation into the enigma posed by the crime via an investigating protagonist, whilst a parallel narrative told through flashbacks gradually reveals the murder itself. The two temporal strands come together in a single narrative line in the resolution – here the trial – where 'truth' is revealed, via the investigator's explanation, to both characters and audience. For John G. Cawelti, this 'classic' detective narrative (1997: 6) constitutes a fable in which crime is revealed as resulting from the 'specific and understandable motives of particular individuals'. It can therefore be dealt with without questioning 'the fundamental soundness of the social order' (ibid.: 12). In Ermarth's feminist analysis, as we have seen, this is an order identified with linear and progressive temporality, power and its association with rationality, and the autonomous (male) subject.

The investigative narrative of *A Question of Silence*, however, is undercut from the film's outset. It begins conventionally, with Janine receiving a phone call – she and her lawyer husband (Eddie Brugman), who first takes the call, answer identically with the non-gendered 'Van den Bos' – and then driving to the scene of the interrogations she is to undertake. She is the active and mobile investigator, crossing space and driving the narrative forward, and we see the prison through her eyes as she approaches, in one of the film's rare point-of-view shots. Once there, still moving purposefully through the space of the prison, she is given details of the crime by the police officer in charge (Kees Coolen); later, this investigative mobility will be repeated in her meeting with the pathologist (Onno Molenkamp). Yet Janine is never in control of either the gaze or the discourse of which she is the ostensible subject. The police inspector patronises and talks over her, already presuming the outcome of her investigation. 'It's an open and shut case . . . There's no doubt about it. They're completely crazy . . . You can spot them a mile away', he says, stepping in front of her at the prison's reception desk. 'I assume you're usually assigned to women. What will you do with these three?', he continues, without waiting for an answer. The pathologist barely acknowledges her. Within the prison, surveillance cameras track Janine's movement down endless identical corridors, and we watch her through the eyes of their male operators, a small black-and-white image relayed on banks of screens, in a journey that now seems both fractured and directionless. Even her signature is institutionally captured, copied and stored.

This opening of the investigation is preceded by nine short scenes, bookended by introductions to Janine's domestic situation. Apart from one scene in which the police inspector establishes the charges against the three women and the fact that they do not know each other, these are structured, as Mary C. Gentile has pointed out ([1985] 1991: 398–9), as sets of parallel blocks, in which we are presented with each of the three women in turn. In these, the spaces are confining – the cluttered living room in which Christine sits in semi-darkness with her small child, the overcrowded café in which An serves its male customers and the expansive office in which Andrea occupies so very little space – and time seems suspended. This is time as Berlant's 'impasse' (2011a), or Chatman's 'excessive particularity' (1981). Mundane and sluggish, it is a temporality without progress, a dull present in which the women's lives are experienced in detail as stasis and isolation. The camera circles restlessly within these scenes, as if it, too, is trapped in this suspended time.

This rhyming structure includes, rather than contrasting with, the two domestic scenes centred on Janine. In the first we see her try to distract and arouse her husband as he reads, only to have him repeatedly rebuff her until she takes a pen and draws it down his body, miming a cutting open and foreshadowing the murder we are to see. The second shows us the first of two dinner parties with friends: the men are visually and discursively dominant, the women almost silent, as Janine's husband presents a political analysis of Western society whose relevance to his own domestic situation he fails to see. In both, the camera circles around the domestic space, as it does around the limiting spaces of the three women, so that, whilst we are presented with Janine's professional difference, we are also made to experience the structural parallels in her situation. By the time that the investigative narrative begins, it is already clear that Janine will be object as well as subject of this investigation.

This structural pattern is repeated throughout the film. We see it in the three scenes that depict the women's immediate actions after the murder, in which each performs an act that disturbs the pattern of her life and achieves a brief sense of pleasure and freedom. We see it in a further sequence of flashbacks, in which the everyday experience of the women as one of isolation, invisibility and silencing is further confirmed. In the most striking of these we witness Andrea present her business analysis at a board meeting, to find her words ignored and the meeting continue as if she had not spoken. As the camera closes in on her impassive face, we hear the magnified sound of her spoon against her coffee cup. A man reaches across to silence her hand, and then repeats her analysis. 'Good thinking, Bob,' says the Chair. Finally, we see it in the interviews that Janine conducts with each woman in turn, which do not advance but baffle her investigation, eliciting from the women only responses that she cannot interpret. Christine, remaining silent, draws her entrapment and isolation in a series of stick figures – man, woman and child – confined within boxes; An talks and laughs loudly and without pause; and Andrea ridicules Janine's search for psychological motivation.

If this temporal structure challenges the primacy of the narrative that it ostensibly serves – the narration that Genette sees as narrative's 'temporal, dramatic aspect' (1982: 136) – then the depiction of the murder displaces it further. It is shown through three long flashback scenes, in which Christine, An and Andrea slowly and silently come together and act, watched by four other women. The arena is the feminised public space of the women's clothes shop, owned and monitored by men. Critics have described these scenes as 'ritualistic' (Rich [1984] 1998: 320, Williams 1988: 108, Gentile [1985] 1991: 401, Smelik 1993: 352), 'ceremonial' and 'magical' (Fischer 1989: 292, 3), 'stylized' (Gentile [1985] 1991: 401) and Brechtian (Rich [1984] 1998: 320). Time is slowed, at times stilled altogether, and ambient sound almost inaudible under the discordant electronic score, as the camera slowly circles around first Christine, and then the other women. Hand-held and at eyeline height, it places us amongst the women, trapped, as Christine is trapped, behind the multiple rails of clothes, and then moving in rhythm with the women. When Christine takes a sweater and puts it in her bag, her action is repeated across the shop by the others, and we watch all seven women move slowly around the space, exchanging glances and echoing actions, as they, and we, close in on the shopkeeper. When the murder begins, the rails which seemed to trap Christine form a barrier to his escape and he is encircled. Fischer describes the movement as choreo-graphed, and the configuration of the women as reminiscent of 'the blocking of a gunfight in a Western' (1989: 293). Unlike such a scene, however, the action is both emotionless and curiously centreless. There is no antagonist, and no frenzy or rage; the women do not speak. Their actions are discontinuous, each provoked not by the man who is its object (after the first blow he falls below our eyeline, and remains out of view), but by the preceding action of another of the women. It is both shocking and blackly comic: the women's weapons are the everyday feminised objects of the women's clothing store – coat-hangers, glass shelves, wooden clothes-stands, a wheeled shopping bag. Across the three scenes, static shots are repeated, each pulling us back from the action to observe, as a witness-participant, the collective, encircling stance of all seven women.

Distanced and made strange in this way, the murder scenes function not as resolution to the film's investigative narrative but, as Geetha Ramanathan writes, as its radical 'interruption' (1992: 67). The 'narrative is not about the murder', she argues, because unlike in the standard detective narrative, 'the story is not completed when we both see the murder and know the motive' (ibid.: 65). There is no explanatory link with the scenes of the women's lives or their responses to Janine, and we are not invited to identify with them through point-of-view shots. We are, however, placed *with* them, positioned as witness-participants in a time-space that operates at the distanced level of ritual or myth,[6] yet is occurring not elsewhere, but in the interstices of the everyday. Instead of reaffirmation of the social order what we find in this revelation of the murder is, as Ramanathan suggests (ibid.: 59), the emergence, as possibility, of 'another story'. The murder is the point at which the women's lives intersect, and it is this mutual recognition, not the murder itself, on which the camera focuses, and in which it progressively involves us. It is a decentring furthered in the scenes in which Janine plays back the recordings of her interviews with the women. At first frustrated in her efforts to determine individual motivation from their responses, she gradually begins to *listen*. The camera centres her in the frame, but it is the women's voices that carry authority – at several points they provide continuity across scenes – so that Janine's home office becomes a shared, communicative space. Her gestures – running a hand through her hair, turning her head away – begin to echo those of the women, and when her husband appears, his sudden presence within the frame seems to violate her space. The camera remains on Janine, pushing him outwards from the frame.

This other narrative is not one developed progressively through an investigative gaze, interrogation and rationalising conclusion, but one glimpsed through a series of temporal shifts and breaks, and through an emphasis on mutual looking, gesture and embodied listening. Two scenes in particular mark its emergence. The first occurs after the second dinner party, in which Janine's husband has once more dominated the visual and discursive frame, speaking to his male guest whilst the two women are once more silent, exchanging only occasional glances. This time, Janine has not attempted to join his political analysis; instead, in an echo of Andrea's disturbance of the board meeting through non-discursive *noise*, we hear the sound of crockery crashing. Afterwards we see Janine sitting reflectively in front of her bedroom mirror. As her husband once again ignores her non-response to his monologue and urges her to bed, we see a momentary image of the three women standing over the fallen shopkeeper. The image is repeated in flashes four times as Janine's husband ignores her 'Don't' and proceeds to have sex with her. The final image occurs after a rapid montage of shots of all four women turning their heads over a cacophony of judgemental male voices. This image is slightly different: the three women now look back, smiling, but our view of them is partly blocked by the backs of two large, uniformed male figures which stand at either side of the frame. Behind the three women, we can now see the four silent witnesses to the murder, also facing us. After a further rapid montage of Janine's turning head, we see her wake, distressed. She goes downstairs to listen to the women's recorded voices.

These images are quite literally flashbacks, but their source is uncertain. They seem to be flashes of Janine's consciousness, but the women look back at *us*, too, and it is our view of the women, as well as Janine's, that is partially blocked in the final image. They are composites, not quite attributable to Janine. The women are wearing the clothes that Janine saw them in, not those of the murder scenes, yet they stand in the shop that we, but not Janine, saw, and both shopkeeper and witnesses are those of the murder. The first image appears when Janine looks in the mirror, and the others when her body is most explicitly, and vulnerably, marked as female. They are images, then, that address us as women, operating in an imaginative space that is shared. They present us with glimpses of both a mirror and an invitation into a fantasised reclaimed space: one which we, like Janine, cannot quite reach.

The second scene is the final scene before the trial. Janine has visited An, whose frustration has exploded into a despairing destruction of her prison room; and Christine, who has spoken for the first time after Janine has stopped questioning and instead communicated through touch, gently turning Christine's face towards her. Now, in her final meeting with Andrea, touch is once more central, and Janine remains silent. Andrea slowly traces the outline of Janine's face and body, closely but without quite touching, before standing to face her. There is no shot/reverse shot; their gaze is mutual, and they share the frame. The scene is ended by the sound of a door opening and a man's voice saying, 'Sorry. Wrong door'. The two women break apart and look towards him. The scene has several resonances. Most obviously, its tender, restrained eroticism contrasts with the heterosexual sex we have recently witnessed. But it also suggests the possibility of a shared looking, a closeness centred on vulnerability and touch, and the centrality of embodiment to subjectivity. It is the shape of Janine's female body that Andrea traces, and it is this that Janine, if she is to speak, must learn to speak from.

The trial is a performance of institutionalised male structural and discursive power. Judges and counsel are men, symbolically robed, whilst women sit in the dock and gallery as silent audience. The only woman to speak is Janine. The camera, however, once more circles the space, catching the shared glances between women – the witnesses to the murder are all present – and marginalising the men in its framing. Janine begins by speaking from within the discourse of psychiatry, whilst the prosecuting counsel

Figure 1.1 Andrea and Janine

offers a series of lurid rhetorical images: 'Was the body not so mutilated, as if a high-heeled army of Furies had viciously inflicted . . .'; 'These three women then indulged, no, wallowed, in the butchery of the proprietor of the boutique'. Yet it is Janine whose objectivity is questioned ('The expert witness is stating personal opinions incompatible with . . . .'), so that she is addressed now as Dr van den Bos, now as *Mrs* Van den Bos. She cannot, it is clear, speak as both a psychiatrist and a woman and remain, in Judith Butler's words, 'socially intelligible'.

Butler uses the term to describe the way in which we are enabled to act – to be recognised as subjects – by social norms that also determine the limits of our agency (2004b: 41). It is also a phrase echoed in Lauren Berlant's argument that the overlapping categories of genre and gender are 'the two clarifying institutions of social intelligibility' (2011a: 176). Berlant's definition of genre includes both lived and fictional practices, so that we can apply it here to both the institutional process of the trial and the fictional detective narrative, both of which should be resolved with Janine's pronouncements on the women's (in)sanity and motives. Instead, speaking, she says, as both a psychiatrist *and* a woman, she pronounces the women 'completely sound of mind' and insists on the importance of gender to an understanding of their actions – and in doing so renders herself socially and generically unintelligible. When, in response, the prosecuting counsel announces that he can see no difference between this case and that of three men killing a woman – restating the irrelevance of gendered power structures to the concept of the legal subject – the women's laughter prevents any resolution. As the laughter spreads to include both Janine and the witnesses to the murder – and perhaps members of the cinema audience for, as in the murder scenes, we are invited to be witness-participants – we are reminded of the congruity between these genres, institutional and fictional, as narrative structures which affirm both the existing social order and the autonomous male subject at its centre. Laughter, as Butler (2019) reminds us, is a bodily eruption (we *break into*

Figure 1.2 The laughter

laughter, *split* our sides, *burst out* laughing) that has the 'power to disrupt public functioning'. It expresses at the level of the body both a shared and vulnerable sociality – contagious laughter makes us permeable to one another – and a resistance to not being heard. Butler calls it a 'somatic break with subjection'. Here, its bodily eruption connects women, and disrupts the progression of institutionally authorised masculine genres. The women must be removed in order that these narratives can be concluded.

Gorris's film, writes B. Ruby Rich in her review, is a 'fantasy'. Women 'do not kill men in our society; overwhelmingly, men kill women'. ([1984] 1998: 323). This is true of both social and fictional generic narratives. *A Question of Silence* appeared at a moment when the most prominent Dutch director was Paul Verhoeven and the dominant popular cinema, that of America, was, as Susan Jeffords (1994) has argued, obsessed with the 'hard bodies' of masculine white men, with the US president borrowing from their narratives for his political rhetoric. These were films in which violence was repeatedly inflicted on the vulnerable female body but in which these bodies were insignificant, except in triggering the hero's revenge, and often anonymous. *Death Wish II, Rocky III* and *First Blood,* the first of the Rambo films, all appeared in 1982, and the fourth Dirty Harry film, *Sudden Impact,* a year later. The *Die Hard* and *Lethal Weapon* franchises were to begin in the next few years. Gorris's film can be seen, then, as a performative act of the kind that Barbara Herrnstein Smith (1981) describes in her account of narrative, a response to these dominant stories. Rejecting the 'hidden order of things' which organises the 'deep structure' of the generic detective narrative, it also refuses its temporal ordering. Instead, it suggests the possibility of another story, one built upon the different lived, liveable and fantasised times of women's experience. It is, as earlier feminist commentators argued, a narrative of resistance, one based on a shared recognition of vulnerability and embodiment. For Elizabeth Deeds Ermarth, with whom I started this chapter, this unsettling of 'meaning and subject' needs to be articulated as discourse if its power is to be fully realised. Gorris's film ends in silence, in an unspoken communication between Janine and the four witnesses as they exit the court building. Turning away from her husband's insistent summons, Janine looks towards them, and the film ends on a freeze-frame of her upturned face. The only words spoken in this final scene are those of an anonymous man who shoulders Janine aside on the courtroom steps: 'Look where you're going, cunt'. In her review of the film, Sheila Johnston writes that in spite of the film's bleak narrative ending – despite the women's disruption the trial will be concluded, confirming the established social order – its 'implied sense of solidarity' is nevertheless 'irrationally, perversely . . . exhilarating' (1983: 48). *A Question of Silence* ends without any articulation by Janine of her new understanding. As Johnston's sense of exhilaration makes clear, however, it is in Gorris's film itself, throwing as it does 'the emphasis off what is finished, conclusive, static, identified and on to what is open, playful, mobile, relational', that we find the discursive articulation Ermarth (1989: 45) calls for.

Broken Mirrors (Gebroken Spiegels) (1984)

'Women', as Ruby Rich commented, 'do not kill men in our society; overwhelmingly, men kill women' ([1984] 1998: 323). Rich's explanation for why *A Question of Silence* should be seen not as the programme for action that critics like Milton Shulman saw in it but as 'a fiction . . . [a] fantasy', also points us towards the subject matter of Gorris's second film, *Broken Mirrors* (*Gebroken Spiegels*). Neil Sinyard, indeed, in one of the few critical discussions of the film, sees it as Gorris's response to reviewers' reactions to the earlier film. 'Okay, if you don't accept the metaphor of *A Question of Silence*', he imagines her as saying, 'I'll show you . . . how patriarchy really operates' (1997: 111). In support, he points to Gorris's use of three of the central actors from *A Question of Silence* (Edda Barends, Henriëtte Tol, Eddie Brugman) in what he describes as 'roles that are more extreme versions of their parts in the earlier film'[7] (ibid.), and to the reversal of the outcomes of violence across the two films: the male perpetrators in *Broken Mirrors* are subject to no investigation or punishment. 'We are dealing with metaphor in *Question*', he writes, 'and actuality in *Broken Mirrors*' (ibid.: 113).

The narrative strategies of the two films, however, have marked similarities. Like *A Question of Silence*, *Broken Mirrors* juxtaposes, parallels and ultimately connects two narratives. The first is a 'thriller' narrative in which a serial killer (Eddie Brugman) abducts, starves to death and finally disposes of the body of an Amsterdam housewife (Edda Barends), charting the process in a series of photographs displayed on the wall of her prison; the film opens with his dumping of the body of his previous victim. The second follows the routine lives of a group of sex workers – Ellen (Coby Stunnenberg), Dora (Henriëtte Tol), Francine (Marijke Veugelers), Jacky (Hedda Oledzky), Irma (Carla Hardy), Tessa (Arline Renfurm), Linda (Anke van 't Hof) and Diane (Lineke Rijxman) – in an Amsterdam brothel, Club Happy House. It is a routine which absorbs the induction of Diane, who needs to earn money to support her young child, the suicide of Linda, the overwhelming influx of a large cohort of celebrating students, and finally the brutal stabbing of Irma in a sudden and unexplained act of male violence. The film closes with the resumption of the brothel's morning routine. Released after the success of *A Question of Silence* at international festivals, including the New Directors/New Films Festival in New York, and following that film's successful distribution in Britain by Cinema of Women, *Broken Mirrors* won best feature at the San Francisco International Lesbian and Gay Film Festival but failed to find a distributor in the US (Rich 1998: 316). In Britain, Cinema of Women found themselves outbid for its rights by Thorn-EMI and 'gained the dubious pleasure of watching [the film] disappear from London cinemas with indecent haste' (Root 1986: 222). It remained unavailable on DVD until 2023.

The serial killer narrative

Coined in the mid-1970s by the co-founder of the FBI's Behavioural Science Unit, the term 'serial killer' became quickly identified with a generic narrative widespread across both fictional and non-fictional media forms. Mark Seltzer notes its dissemination across American culture from the 1970s onwards, citing a former FBI agent's suggestion that the antecedents of the Bureau's serial-crime unit lay as much in 'crime fiction' as in 'crime fact' (1998: 16). Its generic characteristics are familiar. The serial killer himself is an anonymous, outwardly 'normal' white man, 'the kind of guy . . . who probably goes to work everyday. Maybe he does something with statistics. An accountant or a clerk' (FBI profile quoted in Seltzer 1998: 16). '[M]onochrome man', he 'just kind of melts into the city scene' (ibid.: 20). His killings are planned, precise. Beneath the surface, however, lies a monster, psychosexually confused and narcissistic. He may be obsessed, writes Seltzer, with 'mirroring and photographing and filming' (ibid.: 20). His cinematic antecedent is Mark Lewis (Carl Boehm) in Michael Powell's self-reflexive *Peeping Tom*

(1960), a shy and 'ordinary'[8] camera operator – he wears a duffle coat and navigates London on a motor scooter – whose weapon is a knife attached to one of the camera's tripod legs, and who films his victims as he kills them. His victims, who must watch themselves die in a distorting mirror attached to his camera, are sexually active young women, sex workers or actresses, engaged in erotic display. Like Hitchcock's Norman Bates, however, Mark's sexual identity is confused, and he both kills and identifies with his victims. Helen Stephens (Anna Massey), the one potential victim who survives, indeed who challenges and interrogates Mark, is not sexually active.

Helen, then, is the forerunner of Carol Clover's 'final girl' (1992: 35), the smart, boyish, non-sexually active young woman who perhaps defeats and certainly survives the serial killer. Clover's study of the 'slasher' film enumerates its elements (ibid.: 23–4), elements we find established in the serial killer films which emerged and flourished in the late 1970s–early 1980s. The serial killer appears 'normal' – he is an office worker in *Eyes of a Stranger* (1980), an anonymous jilted fiancé in *He Knows You're Alone* (1980), a detective in *The Eyes of Laura Mars* (1978), a doctor in *Dressed to Kill* (1980) and a physicist in the most notorious of these films, *New York Ripper*[9] (1982). He is, however, psycho-sexually disturbed, perhaps because of previous hurt by a woman (*He Knows You're Alone, The Eyes of Laura Mars, New York Ripper*), sadistic and voyeuristic (*Eyes of a Stranger, He Knows You're Alone, The Eyes of Laura Mars*). His victims are sexually active and engaged in erotic display: they include fashion models, strippers, erotic dancers, unfaithful wives and fiancées. The murders take place either in the apparent safety of the victim's home or in what Clover calls a 'Terrible Place': a dark cellar or tunnel-like room. The camera tracks the killer through city streets, without showing his face, but adopts his point-of-view through use of a subjective or I-camera as he stalks his victims. Mirrors and photographs surround the victims and are smashed during the final confrontation, but they also reaffirm the survivor's (sexual) identity at the close of the film. At the end of *Eyes of a Stranger*, for example, the serial killer (John DiSanti) attacks teenage Tracy (Jennifer Jason Leigh), who is blind and deaf, in her kitchen and bedroom. Regaining her sight, she shoots him and enters her bathroom, where we see her first inspect her face and then fondle her breasts, in apparent recognition of her now-adult sexual attractiveness. As she does so, the killer suddenly reappears. Tracy is rescued by her sister Jane (Lauren Tewes), the investigative figure of the film, who, picking up the gun that Tracy dropped, shoots the killer. He falls backwards, smashing the mirrored bath screen. A similar bathroom scene closes *Dressed to Kill*, where the naked and apparently self-pleasuring survivor is once more (slowly) stalked by the killer – we watch her through his eyes – this time to wake screaming from what we learn is a dream.

Seltzer makes clear that this generic narrative has dominated US conceptions of the non-fictional serial killer as well as his cinematic counterpart. Fact and fiction have, he writes, 'a way of changing places here' (1998: 16). In the UK, key aspects of the narrative were conspicuous in media coverage of the Yorkshire Ripper, Peter Sutcliffe, who murdered or attempted to murder twenty women between 1975 and 1980, a period during which Gorris was a drama student in Britain.[10] Joan Smith records the failure of West Yorkshire police to catch Sutcliffe, despite numerous indicators of his guilt. Because they believed him to be a killer of 'prostitutes' and not 'innocent girls', she writes (1989: 127) – the terms are those of a senior West Yorkshire detective – they failed to see 'that these were crimes directed against *women*' (ibid.: xviii). Looking for his monstrous difference, they failed to identify him in the 'ordinary bloke' who was married and 'living in a semi-detached house in a good suburb of Bradford' (ibid.: 118). Smith notes the thematic parallels between media coverage of the Sutcliffe case and its fictional generic counterparts, whose 'clear message', she argues, is that sexually active women '*deserve* to have these things happen to them' (ibid.: 20). In response, she reports, women in the north of England picketed cinemas 'showing films like *Dressed to Kill* and *He Knows You're Alone*' (ibid.: 17).[11]

Broken Mirrors begins with credits picked out in red against a black screen, discordant music suggesting the thriller narrative to come. Against a stark industrial background we see a car drive up onto a deserted foreshore at night. The colour in this opening scene is muted, almost monochrome, as it remains throughout the scenes of this narrative thread. Dumping and then displaying the trussed body of a woman, we see a man then take out a camera from inside his coat, in a movement that echoes the opening of *Peeping Tom*, and take a photograph of the body he has carefully positioned. In later scenes we track the same figure as he follows a mother picking up her children from school, and later as she leaves an evening class and returns home. The red of her coat is bright against the washed-out colours of the street scene. The camera is hand-held and low angle; we do not see the killer's face. In noir-thriller fashion, we view him through the vertical struts of industrial buildings or interior office staircases, and we follow him until he suddenly appears in front of us and his victim, rapidly knocking her unconscious and bundling her into his car. The later scenes see her chained to an iron bed in a lock-up without electricity or light, her progressive starvation charted in a series of photographs which match the three completed sets of eight on the wall opposite the bed. The killer does not speak and remains anonymous.

Broken Mirrors, then, deploys key elements of the serial killer genre. The killer is anonymous and apparently 'normal': we see him in his office building and at home – like Sutcliffe he is married and lives in a semi-detached house in a 'good suburb'. We track him as he stalks his victims through the dark shadows of city streets. He imprisons them in a 'Terrible Place', and records their progressive decline in photographs which he then displays; he follows a pattern in disposing of and arranging their bodies. Reviewing the film, Pam Cook saw these elements as problematic, too similar to sequences in 'thrillers of the Hitchcock/de Palma variety', and wanted Gorris to have 'investigated further the sadist's desire to trap and control his victim' (1985: 114). There are, however, key differences. If in the early scenes the camera tracks the killer, it never views the victim through his eyes – one early scene appears to show us his view of the housewife, before the camera pulls away to reveal that we are watching *him* follow her. Unlike in *Peeping Tom*, we do not see what he sees before he takes his photographs; we see only his attempts to master and control through a repetitive fixing into images, images which are then arranged into the same linear pattern. In the scenes of her imprisonment, our focus is always on the housewife and her attempts to understand her situation. Philip Simpson writes that the serial killer's crimes are 'mechanical and repetitive', and argues that such monochromatic repetition is the product of an industrial age (2000: 20). Gorris's film attributes responsibility rather differently: like Sutcliffe in Joan Smith's analysis, the killer's 'deep-seated hatred of women' (1989: xviii) is shared by the culture around him. As the serial killer narrative thread develops, however, it is increasingly clear that the killer's images, and the fixed, repetitive narrative they construct, tell us nothing about the women they purport to document, and it is the women, not the killer's desires, that concern the filmmaker.

Club Happy House

Most important, the film juxtaposes this attempt to master and control against another very different kind of repetition: one that is allied to community, care and resistance. For, despite the fact that it opens the film, the serial killer story is not its major narrative thread. *A Question of Silence* developed its 'other story' of shared recognition and resistance through temporal shifts and breaks, in fragmentary sequences which interrupted the investigative narrative. In *Broken Mirrors* the aesthetic contrast works differently. It is the serial killer narrative that is stylised and distanced from us, wrapped as it is in another familiar but far more domestic genre, that of the 'woman's film'.

In their influential accounts of the Hollywood genre aimed at a female audience and prominent from the 1930s to the 1960s, both Mary Ann Doane and Tania Modleski draw attention to the films' temporal structure. These are films, writes Doane, 'dominated by duration and repetition' (1987: 106). Centred on interior spaces, domestic and claustrophobic, they are inhabited by women who fail to articulate their desires and whose primary 'activity' is that of waiting; they 'witness departures and arrivals', comments Doane, 'but there is little or no progression' (1987: 107). The women at their centres are silenced, but the desires they fail to express return through music or *mise en scène,* through fantasies of 'events that do not happen', or through bodily performance and excess (Modleski 1987: 327 –35). Both Doane and Modleski draw on Kristeva's concept of 'women's time' to explain the 'insistently repetitive or cyclical' structure of the films (Doane 1987: 193; Modleski 1987: 330), though both are uneasy with the assumption implicit in Kristeva's formulation: that women are positioned outside history. However much these films might seem to speak to a marginalised and separate women's culture, writes Doane, they are patriarchal texts. This is a genre that 'returns to us the familiar scenarios of waiting, giving, sacrificing, and mourning' (Doane 1987: 180), at the expense of attributing to its female protagonists either agency or subjectivity.

The woman's film, then, gives expression to but simultaneously contains women's desires and anger, a theme also emphasised by Lauren Berlant in her studies of the 'female complaint'. To complain is to resist the 'messages and practices of patriarchal dominance' (1988: 245), she writes, but it is also to remain within the structures and performance of normative femininity. For Berlant, 'Women's genres' function as '"safety valves" for surplus female rage and desire' (ibid.), their circular structure ensuring 'consciousness without politics' (ibid.: 252). In contrast, David Greven's more recent queer reading of the genre is, as he writes (2011: 34), far less 'skeptical', and though it is the analyses by feminist scholars that I want to emphasise here, I do want to draw on his argument that 'the chief themes of the woman's film [are] transformation and female vengeance' (ibid.: 182), with the figure of the avenging Fury acting as bridge between this genre and what he sees as its successor: the female-centred horror film. It was the mythical figures of the Furies that were evoked by the prosecuting counsel in *A Question of Silence,* and the Fury as image of trans-formation and vengeance reappears, though very differently, in *Broken Mirrors.*

Greven distinguishes between masquerade – the conventional appearance of femininity that women must perform in order to evade negative judgement – and transformation. The first is 'damaging, wounding' for women; the second, though it may make use of masquerade *en route,* is liberatory, and permits the expression of women's anger (2011: 32–3). *Broken Mirrors* shows us feminine masquerade as a strategy of survival and is deeply sceptical of myths of transformation and their origins. But it also provides another source of resistance in the relationships between the women of Club Happy House, in a series of scenes whose temporal rhythm, one of repetition, waiting, enduring, maintaining – all forms of time's suspension that, in the words of Lisa Baraitser, 'tell us something about care' (2017: 3) – undermines the (imaginary) male narrative of the 'Happy House' visit, but is the heart of the film. Unlike in the woman's film of Doane's characterisation, these scenarios of suspended time are where we find both agency and subjectivity.

Early scenes in the film show us the women's preparations for what Dora calls the lunchtime 'rush hour': 'All present and correct', she says; 'Long live the storm troops'. Surrounded by Club Happy House's many mirrors, we see the women change their clothes and hairstyles, apply makeup and gauge the probable effectiveness of their work. In contrast to the serial killer scenes, the colours here are saturated and rich. 'Irma, you're a picture', says Dora, 'an exquisite beauty!', before embracing her. The tone, reassuring but also ironic, joking, gives the flavour of these scenes. With their shared glances, jokes and comforting touches and embraces, these are moments when masquerade is consciously assumed, but also moments of care into which we as spectators are invited, with the camera repeatedly positioning us as part of the circle of women in long, extended takes. In one scene for example, as opening time for Club Happy House approaches the camera circles slowly within the room as if one of the women, pausing on withdrawn, reflective faces, individual gestures of comfort or humour, silent routines of preparation. Then the doorbell rings, lighting and music change and the women assume their silent poses as static, stereotyped, separated objects available for male choice and male pleasure. 'I almost didn't recognise you', says Diane upon meeting Dora's assumed persona. Later, Dora will perform for her an explanatory masquerade of orgasm whilst an oblivious male client standing at the bar recounts in monologue his version of the narrative of prostitution: 'They were good listeners. Really interested in you. You could see that'. He is structurally powerful, and his voice dominates, but the camera focuses on the women.

This is masquerade as survival. The distance from the constructed image which Dora repeatedly demonstrates is a means not of rendering that image readable, as in Doane's ([1982] 1991) account of cinematic masquerade – these women are fully aware of the images they construct – but of retaining as much agency as possible within a structure in which they are abused. It is a structure that prevents any real communication between men and women, as we see when Diane is faced with a client who lies, curled like an infant, weeping on the bed. She reaches out a hand to him, then withdraws it. The women, however, unalike and emotionally isolated as they are, support one another through bodily and emotional pain by jokes, touch and physical expressions of care.

Transformation, both physical and emotional, is for Greven central to the woman's film. In *Broken Mirrors* this centrality is referenced in a number of ways. It is referred to most directly in the scene following Linda's suicide, when the women celebrate her life in a nearby restaurant. Linda, we have seen, was emotionally and physically vulnerable, defending her pimp ('He's my *friend*') after he had broken her wrist and then sent her back to work. Her naiveté is parodied, with affection, in the Frog Price story[12] begun by Diane but continued by all the women:

> Diane: Kiss a frog? Our princess didn't think much of that.
> Dora: But no luck. The frog remained a fat, green, bloated, slimy toad.
> Diane: And her father kept saying, 'Kiss the frog, my child. Kiss the frog.'
> All: Kiss the frog. Kiss the frog ...
> Ellen: I've kissed many princes, but they all turned into frogs.
> Irma: To Linda!

The fairy tale's promise of the transformative power of romance is revealed to be not a product of female fantasy – Modleski's fantasies of 'events that do not happen' – but a patriarchal ploy to impose control, as feminist writers have also suggested.[13] Belief in it resulted, in Linda's case, not in reassurance but in death. Its divine equivalent is treated more sympathetically, but is seen to be no less illusory. The film's third, and minor, narrative strand shows us Dora's relationship with the reclusive André (Wim Wama), an old man who lives in a hut on waste ground beside the canal where she moors her houseboat. André is never seen – he and Dora do not touch – but we hear his voice speaking of God and the Virgin Mary, and quoting from the Song of Solomon ('Lo, the winter is past ... The flowers appear on the earth') and Corinthians ('We shall not all sleep/ But we shall all be changed').[14] A man wholly without power, he and Dora provide mutual support until his fantasy of divine transformation is abruptly ended with his removal by the Health Department, following a complaint by a neighbour (Elsje de Wijn) in an adjacent apartment. 'I did my duty. He wasn't normal. Old people need protecting', she says when Dora arrives home to find him gone and his hut demolished.

It is transformation via female *rage* on which Greven's revisionist view of the woman's film centres, however. The figure of the Fury, he writes, manifests 'as a result of some kind of blow or deeper wound to a woman's life and sometimes to her body', and produces a retaliation against oppression (2011: 68–9). In Gorris's reworking of the genre, however, this focus on individual transformation is replaced by an emphasis on a mutually sustaining resistance – resistance as a mode of living, or dying – and Greven's climactic act of violence by repetition, and a slowing of time and movement. Time stutters and slows as the women steel themselves for the performance of sexual availability that they will soon have to deliver, or as they sit, spent, in its aftermath. Its rhythms are endlessly repeated – the preparations, the words and actions for clients, the exchange of cash, the cleaning both before and after, Linda's suicide attempts, the unseen Helene's excuses, Francine's threats. Even Diane's final confrontation with the man that we now realise is the serial killer, which most recalls the figure of the Fury, is a repetition of an earlier confrontation with another aggressive client. He, too, tried to insist on service from the women; he, too, carried the threat of violence but manifested his power in the confident, smiling display of his wallet. Diane's actions in response are not a rage-filled 'lashing out' (Greven 2011: 69) but slow, dreamlike, choreographed.

Broken Mirrors, then, shifts our focus from the forward movement of narrative – what Genette termed its 'temporal, dramatic aspect' (1982: 136) – to those moments before and after the actions initiated by the men which 'suspend the course of time' (ibid.: 137), and does it by referencing the tropes of the woman's film. That this narratively interstitial time, a time which 'does not flow' but is corporeally endured, can also be a time when care is manifest and relationships between women established we see throughout the scenes in Club Happy House, and particularly in the developing relationship between Dora and Diane. In one sequence in particular, as they subvert and appropriate the heterosexual conventions of dance ('Do you come here often?' 'What is often?'), time is stilled and an alternative erotic emerges.

In the parallel narrative of the nameless, imprisoned housewife we also see another possibility. In the cramped, imprisoning, abject space in which she finds herself, 'interiority', in Baraitser's words, 'is . . . lived as endurance' (2017: 65), but subjectivity can still be fully realised. In its final sequence, six and a half minutes long with the central section a single, extended shot, she barely moves. Indeed the sequence begins with her reduced to the polaroid images with which the killer has recorded his victims. From the montage on the cell's wall we can see that only the final image in the repeated sequence, that taken after each woman's death and display, remains to be taken. Hers is a world in which time has stopped. 'What day is it today?' she asks; 'I've been here so long.' Deprived of historical time, she is reduced to the abject body: 'I stink .... I'm lying in my own filth.' Yet what the scene registers is not the climax of a thriller narrative but a slow reclaiming of dignity and the coming to consciousness of a subjectivity that transcends its surroundings and speaks directly to us. The killer remains non-individualised, increasingly simply an irritating blockage to our view of her face, as, now fully aware, she answers her own questions: 'Why? What do you want?' 'You hate me, don't you' she concludes, 'so intensely, so terribly', but then corrects herself: 'Us'. As Anneke Smelik notes (1993: 360), in these moments in which the camera focuses on her face with its growing awareness, the muted, almost monochrome tone of this narrative thread is slowly suffused with colour. At the conclusion of the scene, as she closes her eyes and refuses to respond to his increasingly desperate provocations ('You disgust me . . . I'm not going to beg any more . . . plead any more. Not for you.'), silence and passivity become, in these extreme circumstances, markers of resistance.

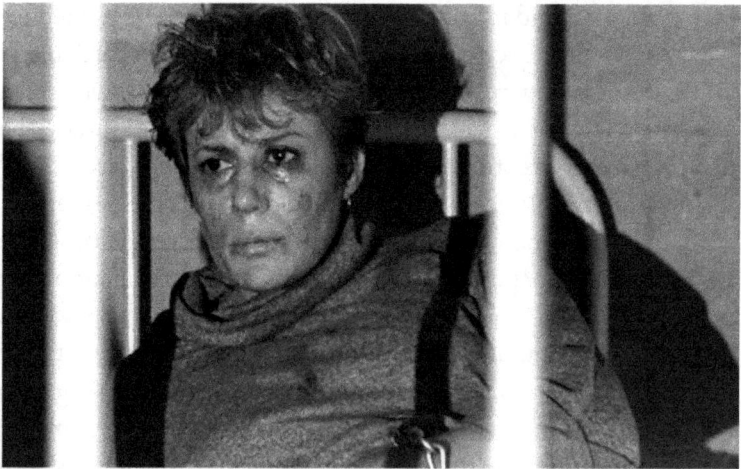

Figure 1.3 The housewife

The ending of the film, like that of *A Question of Silence*, brings the two narrative threads together. The stabbing of the sexually active woman found in the serial killer film occurs not in *Broken Mirrors'* serial killer narrative strand but in Club Happy House. It is unprovoked and unexplained and carried out by one of a group of men who leave without retribution. Dora and Diane's return journey from the hospital, where they and the injured Irma have been driven by a customer labelled by Francine early in the film as 'nice . . . Gives me no trouble', has already pointed up the connections between the narratives. Hearing on the car radio of the discovery of the housewife's body, Dora comments: 'Being an ordinary housewife isn't much safer than being a tart'. When on their return to Club Happy House the customer refuses to leave and instead silently takes out his wallet and offers increasing amounts of money, our view of his action mirrors exactly the shots in which the serial killer drew out his camera. Money and camera, as Anneke Smelik comments (1993: 361), are twin markers of patriarchal power, and if we now realise that this 'nice' customer is also the serial killer, it is equally clear that his identity is unimportant. This 'monochrome man' who 'just kind of melts into the city scene' is, unlike the serial killer of Seltzer's designation (1998: 20), not the mask behind which hides an extraordinary monster. His violence and voyeurism are one with the wider violence that we witness, the product of a patriarchal power structure that, like the distorting mirror wielded by Powell's Mark Lewis, imposes its own images but fails to see women at all.

As he stands, smiling, with money in his hand, the camera positions the killer first beside a mirror in which is reflected a close grouping of three of the women, and then with his back to us, the circle of women ranged before him, as they ranged before the brothel owner in an earlier shot. In both shots he dominates the frame. Diane's slow walk towards him from the group of women is also made in silence, but accompanied on the soundtrack by Haydn's 'Stabat Mater', which gradually increases in volume. Bowing her head, in a pose which echoes images of the Pietà, she picks up the Club's gun from the bar as the soprano voice begins. It is now Diane who fills the frame, and the camera moves with her towards the man. The film, then, reverses the hymn's meaning – this woman is not worshipping her dead son but wielding a gun – but also, in Diane's slow, deliberate movements choreographed to Haydn's music, carries its weight of authority. After a warning shot the killer flees, and Diane slowly turns the gun first on the mirror that carries her own reflection, then on the brothel's remaining mirrors in what Smelik has called 'a ritualistic act of resistance against the male gaze' (2023: 14).

This rupturing of the enclosed world in which the feminine masquerade was performed for male pleasure not only expels the killer but opens the possibility of a move away from the circularity that Berlant identifies with 'the feminine project' (2008: 20), and that is manifest as much in the serial killer genre as in the woman's film. It is a circle in which for Berlant resistance and containment co-exist, finding their entwined expression in the female complaint, voiced so often in the film by Dora. After the shooting Diane and Dora prepare to leave the brothel. 'Are you coming back?' asks Ellen. 'No, never' answers Diane, in a response that seems to promise individual narrative resolution. Dora, however, answers differently:

Figure 1.4 Diane

'Not if I can help it'. The repetitive circularity of male violence and female containment is not so easily broken: the killer remains at large, his violence simply part of the society through which he moves easily, and the film ends as it began, with preparations for another day in Club Happy House.

Writing of the film's two narrative strands, Smelik argues that they 'really tell the same story' (1998: 106), the story which Teresa de Lauretis has deemed the archetypal cinematic narrative. 'Story demands sadism', she writes, quoting Laura Mulvey but reversing her emphasis;[15] it 'depends on making something happen, forcing a change in another person, a battle of will and strength, victory/ defeat, all occurring in a linear time with a beginning and an end' (1984: 132 –3). In it, the woman's function is to wait, accepting or perhaps resisting her confinement within stasis (1984: 139). In Genette's terms, she is an 'ever submissive' function of description, not narration; in Mulvey's, she 'freeze[s] the flow of action' ([1975] 2009: 19). In Gorris's film, however, this doubled narrative with its linear temporality is not our focus. The serial killer, as we have seen, could be any man: we watch him from a distance, curiously, as the camera circles round him; in the serial killer narrative he is never centre screen and there is no ending to his story. The act of violence that disrupts the temporal rhythm of the brothel is random, anonymous and occurs offscreen. It, too, fails to result in victory or defeat. Indeed, stripped of the individualisation and spectatorial involvement that would give it meaning as either heroic or villainous, this story of male sadism is revealed to be itself both repetitive and mundane.

Instead, *Broken Mirrors* asks us to focus, not on the narrative action of the 'temporal, dramatic' (Genette) serial killer story or the disruptive act of violence in the brothel, but on, in Baraitser's words, 'modes of waiting, staying, delaying, enduring, persisting, repeating, maintaining, preserving and remaining' (2017: 2). Although the film, unlike *A Question of Silence*, ends with a relationship established between two of the women, it is not in the promise of any individual narrative resolution that its powerful sense of a resistant agency lies. Rather, it is in those moments of waiting and repetition, when time seems both suspended and expanded, and care and relationality – and in the case of the imprisoned housewife, full subjectivity – emerge. For Butler, vulnerability as a source of community and resistance cannot be conceptualised outside the power structures that both enable and constrain its mobilisation. In *Broken Mirrors*, as in *A Question of Silence*, these structures are evident in both the cinematic world the film creates and the generic structures it deploys and subverts. It is on the possibilities of agency, resistance and care that nevertheless exist, however, that it insists.

Notes

1 Gorris had written the script in 1978 and presented it to Chantal Akerman for Akerman's consideration. Gorris notes:

> 'I did not at first think of directing it myself as I had no experience whatsoever and I thought it would be unlikely anybody would let me. I wrote to Chantal asking if she would consider directing it (I was blown away by *Jeanne Dielman* at the time). She asked me to come and see her in Paris. The script was in Dutch and though she was Belgian she spoke no Flemish. I told her, in English, the whole script from beginning to end. She didn't interrupt once. When I had finished she said: "You have to direct it yourself." And that's about all she said. So I went home and told a potential producer that I wanted to do it myself. (I said the same to an Oscar-winning Dutch director who was interested in directing it. The man had an apoplexy). I would never have had the guts or the self-confidence to direct *A Question* if Chantal had not encouraged me' (Gorris 2024).

With the aid of producer Matthijs van Heijningen Gorris then obtained Dutch government funding for the production. (Root 1986: 215).

2 The phrase is Janine's, speaking to her husband.

3 See especially Jeanette Murphy (1986), Jane Root (1986) and Mary C. Gentile ([1985] 1991).

4 See, for example: Sheila Johnston, *Monthly Film Bulletin* 1 January 1983; Barbara Kruger, *Art Forum* summer 1983; Sarah Lefanu, *Time Out* 18–24 February 1983; Helen Mackintosh, *City Limits* 18–24 February 1983; B. Ruby Rich, *Village Voice* 7 August 1984 (reprinted in Rich 1998).

5 See: David Castell, *Sunday Telegraph* 20 February 1983; Margaret Hinxman, *Daily Mail* 18 February 1983; Jackie Skarvellis, *Morning Star* 18 February 1983; Michael Wigan, *The Scotsman* 21 August 1982; Janet Maslin, *New York Times* 18 March 1983; Richard Cook, *New Musical Express* 4 December 1982.

6 A number of critics (Dittmar (1986), Ramanathan (1992), Smelik (1993), Williams (1988)) compare the murder, with its silent witnesses, to Greek myth or tragedy, Fischer to a Shakespearean tragedy (1989: 293).

7 Edda Barends plays the silent housewife Christine in the earlier film, and the housewife-victim in *Broken Mirrors*, Henriëtte Tol the secretary in *A Question of Silence* and the sex worker Dora in *Broken Mirrors*, and Eddy Brugman Janine's husband in the earlier film and the killer in *Broken Mirrors*.

8 Ian Christie notes the response of *The Spectator*'s Isobel Quigly to the film that it was more disturbing because it seemed 'normal' and 'homely' (1978: 57).

9 This film was refused an exhibition certificate in Britain but was released in Holland in 1982. Its killer stabs and sexually mutilates his victims, including slashing the abdomen and an eye of his final victim – Irma's injuries in *Broken Mirrors*.

10 She graduated with an MA in Drama from the University of Birmingham in 1976.

11 Ironically, however, women in north-east England also picketed a showing by Leeds Animation Workshop of *Broken Mirrors*, on learning that its content included a serial killer victimising women (personal communication from Terry Wragg of Leeds Animation Workshop, 16 June 2023).

12 In the story, first published by the brothers Grimm in 1812, a princess reluctantly befriends a frog, whom she meets when she drops a golden ball into a pond and he retrieves it for her in exchange for her friendship. The frog, who is under a wicked spell, magically transforms into a handsome prince, in most versions when the princess kisses him.

13 See, for example, Anne Sexton, 'The Frog Prince' ([1971] 2001) and Marge Piercy, 'A Story Wet as Tears' (1983).

14 Song of Solomon 2:11-12; 1 Corinthians 15:51

15 See Mulvey ([1975] 2009): 22.

2

Imagining otherwise

If *Broken Mirrors* received very little distribution, *The Last Island* (1990), Gorris's third film, disappeared almost entirely. 'Almost at the same time as the film premiered', reports Gorris, 'the Dutch producers [First Floor Pictures] went bankrupt and the film became almost completely invisible' (2023). The stock was sold, and it was unclear who had bought it.[1] A single print was finally found in the archives of Eye Filmmuseum in Amsterdam by Nico Bruinsma, director of cult and arthouse film distributor Cult Epics. An international screening print (unlike the prints for Dutch distribution, it had no subtitles), it was heavily damaged.[2] Restored by Cult Epics, it was finally released on DVD and Blu-ray in October 2023.

In Anneke Smelik's account of Gorris's early films, she groups *The Last Island* (1990) together with Gorris's first two films as her 'violence trilogy', a grouping which has been followed elsewhere.[3] Each of the three, she writes, 'is situated in a separate world apart from society' (a prison, a brothel, a desert island) which stands as a metaphor for a male-dominated society in which 'power relations explode into violence' (1998: 93). Like her first two films, *The Last Island* is, as Gorris says, a story 'about how women manage to survive in a male dominated society' (2023). For Smelik, however, whereas *A Question of Silence* and *Broken Mirrors* anchor their metaphors in a convincing realism, *The Last Island* fails to be more than allegorical, making its 'political message . . . overbearing' (ibid.: 94). Yet for Gorris herself the film is one of *four* stories that she had written on this theme, *Antonia's Line* (1995) being the fourth. 'In the late seventies', she says, 'I had four ideas for four scripts ; four stories about how women manage to survive in a male-dominated society. Strong women, survivors. Over the years these stories became the four films that I wrote and directed, in the order I had written them' (2023). As with *Antonia's Line* but unlike in her first two films, however, the territory of *The Last Island* is myth rather than realism. It is, says Gorris, 'a sort of end of the world story' (ibid.).

Fantasy, writes Judith Butler, 'is part of the articulation of the possible. ... [It] is what allows us to imagine ourselves and others otherwise', taking us 'beyond what is merely actual and present into a realm of possibility, the not yet actualized or the not actualizable' (2004b: 28–9). Yet solidified as the public fantasy of myth, its narratives have served a very different purpose, consolidating and affirming dominant culture whilst claiming universal, natural or archetypal status. A critical mythopoesis, as Rachel Blau DuPlessis argues (1985: 107), must both contest this affirmative function and re-vision[4] the narratives it authorises. This is, she writes, an act of both 'delegitimation' (of existing narratives) and invention (ibid.: 108), and it is central to the work of the women writers she explores, but it is also hugely difficult. In her discussion of *Antonia's Line*, Geetha Ramanathan addresses these difficulties as they apply to women filmmakers. 'Mythologizing women', she writes, 'whether in epic or film, has not served women well', naturalising 'classical male narrative paradigms' whilst 'robbing [women] of historical agency and indeed historical identity' (2006: 178). To attempt a re-visioning like that of which DuPlessis writes, a woman filmmaker must disrupt 'the smooth chain of male generational storytelling', a task that requires both the 'undoing [of] received mythologies' and the creation of new feminist myths. As with the women writers discussed by DuPlessis, this is often addressed through the 'rewriting' or 'overwriting'[5] of existing myths and genres (Ramanathan 2006: 177). This chapter therefore groups together *The Last Island* and *Antonia's Line* as films which engage explicitly with what Ramanathan calls 'the mythical mode' (ibid.: 179). Whereas *Antonia's Line* is concerned with the question of female mythmaking and how this might rework women's relationship to time and history, however, *The Last Island* is focused on undoing an existing mythical narrative, one deeply implicated in our dominant concepts of temporal and spatial order.

The island myth

Daniel Defoe's *Robinson Crusoe* is a book that from its first publication in 1719 has been a pivotal text for Western civilisation (Volkmann 2011: 131),[6] and in particular for ideals of a Western masculinity manifest through colonial conquest. These major ideological themes, argues Diana Loxley, find their ideal – and idealised – setting in the topos of the desert island, a mythic space of fertility and abundance where all historical and political contradictions can be eliminated (1990: 2–3) and an ideal Western male identity constructed in opposition to an imagined savage primitivism (Volkmann 2011: 132). 'The desert island setting is', writes Loxley, 'the ultimate gesture of simplification' (1990: 3).

Over the two centuries following the publication of Defoe's novel the dissemination of this 'island myth' (Loxley 1990: 3) occurred through countless rewritings, adaptations and imitations in popular and 'children's' fiction – books like Verne's *The Mysterious Island* (1875), Wyss's *The Swiss Family Robinson* (1812), Ballantyne's *The Coral Island* (1858), and Stevenson's *Treasure Island* (1883) – in which 'male heroes, descendants of Robinson Crusoe, made manifest their resourcefulness in struggles on desert islands or the high seas, in confrontations with savages, tyrants and beasts and who, unscathed, brought back to the homeland their tales of adventure'[7] (Loxley 1990: 5). Defoe's text, writes Loxley, 'teaches lessons which are taken to be singular and historically transcendental, true for all time, and which may always be relied upon to reaffirm that we have not lost, and never will lose, either our civilised habits or our greatness' (ibid.): 10).

It constitutes, then, one of the 'classical male narrative paradigms' of which Ramanathan writes.

> But the wonder of the story was, how five such refractory, ill-matched fellows should agree about these women, and that some two of them should not pitch upon the same woman ... (Defoe 1719b: 187)

The above quotation comes from Defoe's *The Farther Adventures of Robinson Crusoe,* one of two sequels that Defoe himself published within a year of the original *The Strange and Surprising Adventures of Robinson Crusoe.* One of the very few references to women in the books, it describes the process by which five colonists draw lots for a woman, and gives us Crusoe's judgement as to which – given that all the captured women are 'most willing, quiet, passive, and subjected Creatures, rather like Slaves than Wives' – should be judged 'the best wife of the parcel' (1719b: 190, 187). His answer is that it is the woman who can be most help in 'application and business' (ibid.: 187). Apart from such brief incidents, women are absent in the Crusoe narratives; Crusoe reports his marriage, and then the death of his wife, in a single sentence. Femininity is represented by the motherland, domesticated and already contained, or by the island itself, seen as either terrain to be conquered or an engulfing dark force (Volkmann 2011: 136). In successfully subjugating it, white masculinity is established through its identification with conquest, with religion, and with work: these heroes achieve dominance through 'self-reliance, perseverance, clear-cut belief systems, and adherence to a religious creed' (ibid.: 132). This, then, is an exclusively male myth;[8] the absence of women is troubled only – and momentarily – by considerations of the future in which 'woman's absent presence is ... felt in [her] ultimate power to give birth' (Loxley 1990: 60).

It is a myth whose dissemination has continued in cinema, from the more than fifteen adaptations of Defoe's novel to twenty first-century incarnations of Crusoe such as Tom Hanks's Chuck Noland in *Cast Away* (2000) or, in more apocalyptic mode, Will Smith's Robert Neville in *I Am Legend* (2007). William Golding's critique of the genre's ideological foundations, *Lord of the Flies* (1954), to which Gorris's film has been compared – Neil Sinyard (1997: 102) calls it 'a feminist *Lord of the Flies* for grown-ups' – was itself re-adapted in 1990, the year of *The Last Island*'s release. Golding's novel is a critical re-working of Ballantyne's *Coral Island* of 1858, in which three shipwrecked boys establish the values of a specifically English colonial masculinity, with its combination of violence ('adventure') and religion, on the desert island on which they find themselves. Unlike Peter Brook's 1963 adaptation, which intensified Golding's critique of a patriarchal Western civilisation seen to be in ruins, the 1990 film works to restore Ballantyne's values, or at least an updated Americanised version of them. Jack is now the bad boy of a group of military cadets, not the upper-class chief chorister with the instinctive sense of command of his class, so that his degeneration into brutal savagery is a betrayal of the forces of civilisation exemplified by parents, teachers and the American military academy, not the revelation of the darkness at its core. Girls are referenced as part of that civilised world ('We got it made: no parents, no teachers, no academy, no girls'), but the casual use of the feminine as insult – '*Miss* Piggy', and 'See you tonight, *girls*' – is definitional. As in the film's nineteenth-century novelistic predecessors, masculinity is here established through its superiority and power over the feminised other.

The Last Island

The Last Island depicts the aftermath of a plane crash from which five men – an English army major, Nick (Kenneth Colley), a Scottish entrepreneur, Sean (Paul Freeman), a French biologist, Pierre (Marc Berman), a young Australian sportsman, Frank (Mark Hembrow), and an American teenager, Jack (Ian Tracey) – and two women – an English-Canadian lawyer, Joanna (Shelagh McLeod) and an elderly Eastern European, Mrs. Godame (Patricia Hayes) – are, apart from a dog, the only survivors. Stranded on a desert island, the seven begin by co-operatively constructing both a mode of living and a boat on which they hope to escape. After the failure of their escape attempt, however, and the growing realisation that they may be the last people alive after an atomic disaster or war, conflict and an increasing violence replace co-operation, and Joanna, as the only woman capable of childbearing, becomes, like Defoe's 'best wife of the parcel', the target for the five men. At the end of the film all five men are dead and Joanna, who may or may not be pregnant, sits with Mrs. Godame and the (female) dog on the beach, looking out to sea. To Joanna's question 'So what do we do next?' Mrs. Godame replies, 'We will finish the boat'.

In a largely critical account of her first four films, Gerdin Linthorst reports that Gorris 'immersed herself in masterpieces of the genre such as *Lord of the Flies, Treasure Island* and *Robinson Crusoe*' in preparation for *The Last Island* (1996: 198). The film contains explicit references to some of these texts: Sean's self-consciously ironic singing of 'Yo ho ho and a bottle of rum' from *Treasure Island,* for example, or Joanna's echo of Peterkin's 'It must be . . . Paradise' from *Coral Island.* The survivors name the dog Tuesday. Jack, the 'tall, strong, and manly' eighteen-year-old 'king' of *Coral Island* and autocratic leader of the choristers-become-hunters in *Lord of the Flies,* is here a nine-teen-year-old American college boy whose aggressively sexual bravado co-exists with a child's desire for comfort. Peterkin, who becomes Simon in Golding's novel (Bufkin 1965: 41), is here the bespectacled Pierre, combining Simon's hatred of violence with Piggy's clumsiness and scientific rationality. The combination of warped religiosity and imperialist violence with which Golding endows Jack is in Gorris's film given to Nick, the English army major whose belief in the righteousness of his fundamental-ist Christianity, and his own mission to impose it, authorises increasingly brutal attacks on all who oppose him. Finally, Gorris's own use of the word 'horror' to describe the film – 'I'm not ready for *Antonia* 's optimism yet. First some horror has to come out' (quoted in Linthorst 1996: 198) – together with the survivors' obsession with building and repairing their boat, recall Conrad's *Heart of Darkness* ([1899] 2007), another, though far more ambivalent, text about white colonial masculinity's encounter with its others.[9] The most 'allegorical' (to use Smelik's term) of the film's characters is, however, Mrs. Godame, who is, as her name suggests, the moral and spiritual counterpoint to the aggressively patriarchal Nick, and who, as a woman, has no counterpart in previous articulations of the island myth. When Sean insists that the survivors must now make their own laws, she responds, 'By all means let us have laws, but laws of love and caring'. Viewed first in an aerial shot in crucifix pose where she has been thrown from the plane during the crash, she is most often seen standing apart: a still, and in the film's early scenes silent, observer. She is given little context: her accent appears to be Eastern European, but we learn only that she is, or has been, a mother. 'I have lost most of my children', she tells Joanna; the other survivors she addresses as 'my child' or 'my son'. Her flaw, she says, is 'despair'.

Writing of Verne's *The Mysterious Island*, Loxley comments on the 'nineteenth-century European appropriation of territory and annexation of space and time' typified by his novels (1990: 18). In these island myths space becomes empty of inhabitants, a paradise awaiting European colonisation, and social and political history is replaced by religiously inflected individual life stories which work to reinstate precisely the social order from which the castaway has come, even as they eliminate its actual historical and political context. Thus Robinson Crusoe, as Laurenz Volkmann writes, 'keeps up the routines of civilized life like regular reading, keeping a diary, maintaining a strict daily routine of keeping things in order, and adhering to rituals that create order and meaning' (2011: 138). Faced with the absence of historical, or clock, time, these shipwrecked patriarchs re-establish its mechanisms over and against both the cyclical rhythms of a seasonal temporality and disruptive natural forces, moving relentlessly forward towards the moment of rescue and return. For Golding's shipwrecked boys it is the loss of linear time and its rituals – school assembly, the licensed permission to speak – that marks the loss of civilisation, history and memory.

This process of 'keeping things in order' characterises the survivors' behaviour at the start of *The Last Island*. They are organised and disciplined, sorting and labelling their findings from the wrecked plane ('cigarettes', 'women's skirts', 'socks', 'razors', 'men's pants' ...), building shelters for different communal and domestic functions – cooking, sleeping, researching – and allocating functions according to existing skills and conventional social and gendered divisions. The rifle is for Nick, the research space for Pierre, and cooking and sewing belong with Mrs. Godame. The boat is designed and built through ordered teamwork, and when Jack thinks he sees a distant plane, the signal fires are already in place and swiftly lit. Joanna, who keeps a diary, also carves a visual record of the number of days and weeks of their stay into the bark of a tree. The island, safely ordered, appears to her as 'paradise'.

The first disruption of these 'rituals that create order and meaning' comes with the arrival of the first of two ghost ships with which the film presents us. This one, a small sailing boat with tattered sails, is washed onshore with a sole occupant whose body is covered in burns and sores. To Pierre's 'Maybe a tanker caught fire' Mrs Godame responds, 'Maybe the world caught fire', and as they burn the boat and its occupant, Sean reflects for the first time, 'I think we're the last people'. If this boat suggests the many ghost ships of

Figure 2.1 'Island paradise'

legend which are harbingers of death, then the extended becalming which precedes the destruction of the survivors' own boat recalls the fate of Coleridge's doomed mariner, held stationary below 'a hot and copper sky'.[10] In *The Last Island*, the becalmed boat is shot against a coppery red sky, before the palette becomes blue-black and the moon is finally enveloped by blackness. Blown back to the island by the force of the storm that follows, the survivors find that it has also destroyed their camp. It is this second event that is decisive in disturbing the assumption of Western civilisation's permanence and coherence that underpins the survivors' attempt to control and manage time. Two key shifts take place. One is an increasing struggle for dominance between Sean, the gay billionaire whose relationships with his young male protégés have, despite their liberalism, been as transactional, as Joanna points out, as her ex-husband's treatment of her ('When I finally left him, he screamed at me, "But I invested in you"') – or as Crusoe's evaluation of women – and Nick, whose patriarchal values are more traditionally based in the combination of Christianity and violence. Nick claims for himself alone the right to kill, and builds a treehouse platform in the jungle from which he can exercise surveillance and control. Sean is increasingly forceful in ridiculing him.

The second shift centres on the most valuable, and disturbing, aspect of woman for the island myth's masculinist fantasies of self-sufficiency: her power to give birth. As hope of a world beyond the island recedes, the men close ranks to demand that Joanna bear the island's future children. Joanna is the first of Gorris's female protagonists to be without a supportive community of women. In our opening view of her she wears a tailored business suit, and she has the confidence of the post-feminist high achiever, unthreatened by Jack's immature macho posturing: 'I can take care of myself', she says, 'and if anyone thinks I'm prepared to be raped meekly, they'd better think twice'. Her closest relationship is with Sean, with whom she is jokingly competitive, and to him she confides that she prefers being alone: 'No hassle'. Towards the elderly Mrs Godame she is merely politely solicitous. She is, then, a woman of what Susanna Danuta Walters calls the 1980s 'so-called "postfeminist" generation' (1991: 104), confident of her individual empowerment in the world of men. It is a generation, writes Walters, which has 'grown up with [the] hard-won right [to 'control over their bodies'], accepting it as a *right*, but seeing it as one which is individually held and exercised, compatible with self-sexualisation, and unconnected to the collective or political. Unlike in Gorris's first two films, the camera does not move fluidly to position us with Joanna as a central female figure: most often it groups the survivors in pairs or larger groups, pulling away to establish a visual distance from them.

Following the wreckage of the first, ordered camp, however, the group divides according to gender: the men gather to discuss Joanna's presumed fertility and the camera follows their appraising gaze, first as a group and then individually in turn. Their motives may differ – Nick claims a God-given right over Joanna's body, Sean is pragmatic, whilst Pierre speaks of the hope that children embody – but their solidarity as a male group with the power of possession over the single fertile woman overrides their differences. Like their nineteenth-century predecessors, these men see the woman's function as procreator of future colonists. Their power is ceremonially played out in the party held to celebrate Joanna's birthday, organised as a formal dance to the accompaniment of a scratchy recording of Glenn Miller's Moonlight Serenade. The dress is black tie, and the men appear in a range of 1950s formal wear, from Pierre's plaid Buddy Holly jacket to the white dress uniform worn by Nick.[11] When Joanna appears out of the darkness, wearing an off-the-shoulder red evening gown complete with decorative fabric flower, and carrying a Japanese parasol, her hair styled in a 1940s roll, she is visually separated from the rest of the group and object of their collective gaze. In the exchanges that follow they compete for her attention, first with presents and then as dance partners. As the scene develops, the gendered power that underpins such social rituals becomes increasingly evident, to us and to Joanna, with the threat of sexual violence implicit not only in Jack's clichéd advances but also in the other men's silent complicity. Mrs Godame sits apart from the group, a silent observer.

After the party, Jack is bitten by a snake – in a black reversal of another paradise myth – as he attempts to assault Joanna, and Nick, ignoring Mrs Godame's 'It's all right Jack . . . It's not poisonous', cuts off his hand.[12] From this point, the gendered opposition is intensified. Forced to listen to Jack's screams as he succumbs to gangrene, the men seek to control his death through a 'mercy killing', whilst the women, his carers, insist on Jack's right to choose the way he will die. In a grotesque parody of democracy the men's votes prevail. When their insistence on Joanna's duty to provide children is renewed following Jack's death, it is again Mrs Godame who articulates the ethical position ('It is better to bring no children onto this island than to force their creation'), whilst the men insist that 'There *must* be life'. To Joanna it is now clear that the men had 'worked it all out . . . . Even before my birthday party' and, like Ellen in *Broken Mirrors* forced to service one of the party of students, she takes the only agency available to her, in choosing the least aggressive of the men, in this case Pierre, as prospective father of her child.

Following Jack's funeral, the leadership contest between the rigidly fundamentalist Nick and the (neo)liberal Sean escalates, and Nick shoots Sean dead. Frank, his lover, feels he must avenge Sean – 'I *owe* him . . . I don't know what else to do' – and sets out to kill Nick. He succeeds, hauling Nick up on to the cross that Nick himself constructed and then piercing his eye with a crossbow, but Frank has himself been fatally wounded. Pierre, who despite his antipathy to violence has belatedly set out to help Frank – 'I must go. Don't you see that' – is also killed. The sequence of events is both grimly inevitable and blackly comic: 'I have to get pregnant for *this*!' protests Joanna. Whilst Nick personifies the 'evil' (Joanna's description) of a messianic patriarchal colonialism, the other men are victims of codes of masculinity that simply do not allow them to act otherwise: to, in Joanna's words, 'live together . . . just live'.

Overwriting the island myth

The Last Island, then, is Gorris's undoing of the island myth. It is easy to see why Smelik saw it as too allegorical, though the same criticism was not made of the versions which Gorris overwrites. For Gorris, herself, however, the reverse is true: filmed on the lush Caribbean island of Tobago, the film lacked, she writes, the quality of estrangement that would have best served it. It 'would have been better', she concludes, 'if we had made it in the studio' (2023). It is Gorris's bleakest film. The disruption of the linear temporality which characterises both history and the heroic narratives of the island myth is here effected not by its displacement by another story, of shared recognition and resistance, as in her earlier films, but by the stilling of time in images that portend disaster. Here, that other story is undeveloped and unheard. We do not see what Joanna writes in her journal, and although after the storm Mrs. Godame responds to Jack's frightened, 'Tell us a story, Mrs. G.' with 'Once upon a time there was . . .', we do not hear the story she tells. Her maternal wisdom and compassionate logic are ignored, she speaks of her own despair, and although the two women argue strongly against the men, they do not form a bond that might narratively or cinematically displace the playing out of the men's story.

Instead, in a series of temporal interruptions – the gothic intervention of the ghost ship; the images of the survivors' own boat becalmed amidst a sea and sky that turn first red and then deep blue, fading to black as storm clouds slowly cover the moon; the surreally anachronistic party sequence; the biblical revenge of Frank – linear narrative movement is halted in the service of an intensifying critique. Played out through these anachronous sequences, it is a critique that reaches back to encompass the cultural history of the island myth and the ideological themes that it expresses. The last of these sequences comes at the end of the film, after the death of Frank, and is identified in part with Joanna's point of view. To the sound of liturgical music sung by a single soprano voice the still surface of the ocean is slowly crossed by the second of the film's two ghost ships. This one contains the seven survivors, all posed in the formal dress of the party. Joanna sits in the prow, and Mrs. Godame in the stern; the men are grouped in the centre, between the two women. All but Joanna face forward, the men looking purposefully outwards, beyond the boat. As it moves across the screen and into the distance the boat fades into light, and the film cuts to Joanna's pensive face. In its music and slow, deliberate movement, the sequence recalls the ending of *Broken Mirrors*, but this sequence is retrospective, and judgemental: this ship of fools,[13] bound together by the ideological values they share, was always doomed.

The two women end the film sitting on the sand together with the dog between them, looking out to sea. The camera circles slowly around them, emphasising their isolation on the now tranquil island. Joanna can now acknowledge Mrs. Godame's wisdom and prescience, suspecting that the old woman foresaw the events we have seen play out. 'How come you always seem to know so much? . . . Am I pregnant then?' she asks. Mrs. Godame answers enigmatically, responding only to the question 'How do you stand it all?' 'I enjoy *life*', she answers; 'There is, after all, nothing else'. They will, they agree, finish the boat, but there seems little possibility of a surviving world beyond the island, and Mrs Godame's final glance across at Joanna expresses only doubt.[14] A genealogy of women, the film suggests, represents the only hope for a rewriting of the island myth and all its ideological underpinnings in a way that might centre 'life', but that hope seems to be a fantasy in which neither woman quite believes.

Figure 2.2 *The Last Island*: ending

Antonia's Line (Antonia)

In an interview with Judith Butler in 1994, Rosi Braidotti outlines to her sceptical interviewer her understanding of Kristeva's concept of 'women's time'. 'Woman', she says, 'is a complex entity which . . . pertains *both* to the longer, linear time of history and to a deeper, more discontinuous sense of time: this is the time of cyclical transformation, of counter-genealogies, of becoming and resistance' (Braidotti, in Butler 1994: 41). It is a concept that despite its problems Braidotti wants to retain for its suggestions of 'embodied genealogies and counter-memories' (ibid.: 42), and at the same time radically de-essentialise. Kristeva's concept should be seen, she insists, as a *description* of the gendered dichotomy that Western culture has constructed between the abstract 'teleological time of historical agency – colonized by men' (ibid.: 41) and the 'situatedness' of women's relationships to temporality, with their cyclicality, repetitions and internal contradictions. It is a situatedness, she argues, that also produces a subjectivity which is both multiple and relational.

This is the subject matter of *Antonia's Line*. Marleen Gorris's fourth film takes up the challenge issued at the end of *The Last Island*: to imagine a genealogy of women which, in Caroline Bainbridge's words, embraces not only 'mothers and daughters' but also 'the horizontal relation of women-among-themselves' (2008: 114), and which centres, as Mrs. Godame insisted, 'life'. 'Life's got to be lived', says Antonia (Willeke van Ammelrooy), echoing Mrs. Godame, for 'This is the only dance we dance'. Despite the fact that like her first two films and unlike *The Last Island* it was a Dutch-language film, *Antonia's Line* was far more successful than its predecessor, winning the Toronto International Film Festival People's Choice award, two Dutch Film Festival Golden Calf awards, Best Director at the Hamptons International Film Festival, Best Screenplay and Audience Choice Award at the Chicago International Film Festival, and the 1996 Oscar for Best Foreign Language Film. Gorris thus became the first female director to win an Oscar for best film. With reviews emphasising its 'warmth' and 'tenderness', its 'magical' and 'poetic' qualities, and its 'lightheartedness',[15] for critics it meant, in the words of Robert Sklar who interviewed Gorris about the film, that she had 'left the dark side of feminism' and embraced its 'lighter side' (1996: 26); she could now be celebrated. The film had been no less difficult to make than *The Last Island*, however. An international co-production, it had, says Gorris, 'three producers [Dutch, English and Belgian] who all wanted to provide as little money as possible and have as much influence as possible', with the result that 'the crew went on strike because they weren't paid'. In marked contrast to the later reviews, after she had finished editing the film, she recalls, 'one of the producers was so disgusted with it, he wanted to do a completely new edit'. It was only because the Dutch producer 'stood firm' that 'my director's cut was released exactly as I had wanted it to be' (Gorris 2023).

Antonia's Line opens with the impending death in old age of Antonia, before taking us back fifty years to the end of World War II and her return, with daughter Danielle (Els Dottermans), to the village where she grew up and where her mother (Dora van der Groen) is about to die. As she settles on the farm that she inherits, the film traces her 'line' across three further generations: her daughter Danielle, granddaughter Thérèse (Carolien Spoor/Esther Vriesendorp/Veerle van Overloop), and great-granddaughter Sarah (Thyrza Ravesteijn). Around this generational line is accumulated a much larger community of lovers and their families, friends, and refugees from the world beyond. The film closes with the return to Antonia's death in the present, and the revelation that the voice-over narration which we have heard throughout the film is the adult voice of Sarah (Lineke Rijxman).

The film, said Gorris in interview, is 'a fable, or a bit of a myth, or a fairy tale' (Sklar 1996: 27), descriptions which were echoed not only by reviewers responding to its multi-generational structure and its elements of magic realism but also, more seriously, by feminist critics. For Kathi Maio it is a 'feminist fable' (1996: 54), for Karen Jaehne a 'matriarchal passion play [with a] utopian agenda' (1996: 27), for Mary Russo 'a fable of female generativity and influence'

(1999: 28), and for Caroline Bainbridge a 'kind of pastoral, feminist fairy tale' (2008: 114). Anneke Smelik (1998: 93) calls it 'a feminist rewriting of the epic genre', whilst Geetha Ramanathan sees it as 'feminist myth' (2006: 178). These designations suggest something of the film's ambition and, as Ramanathan explores, something too of the difficulties it confronts. 'It is easier to depict dystopias than utopias', writes Kathleen Rowe Karlyn, 'to show the horror that exists than to imagine something better' (2011: 239). Moreover myth and fairy tale, as many feminist writers have pointed out (de Lauretis 1984, Hirsch 1989, Walker 1995), have not served women well, from the 'timeless vision[s]' of the singular hero described by Joseph Campbell, whose Oedipal journey through a series of trials set in a magical time and place brings him at last to knowledge, with woman representing 'the totality of what can be known' (Campbell [1949] 1993: 4, 116), to the fairy-tale stories of magical transformation which, as Nancy Walker has commented, remain 'remarkably fixed in their essential elements', with 'the possibilities for female exercise of power . . . extremely circumscribed' (1995: 46). Gorris, as we have seen, had already engaged in critical re-visions of these narratives,[16] and we see this again in *Antonia's Line*, in the witty references to Christian mythology (in addition to Danielle's visions, Antonia is the 'prodigal daughter' and the film's five-generation female lineage ironically echoes that of Genesis), to stories of witchcraft (in Antonia's powerful cursing of the rapist Pitte [Filip Peeters]), and to popular genres (in the confrontation of Antonia with Pitte at gunpoint in the village square or 'the knight on the white charger'[17] who makes Danielle pregnant). Here, however, she goes further. Antonia's framing within 'land and elements, larger than the social or symbolic' suggests the scope of myth, as Ramanathan suggests (2006: 183), conferring 'the authority of lineage and descent' on the stories the film tells (ibid.: 182). Yet these stories refuse both the heroic narratives of myth and their opposites and complements, the monumental cyclicality of a 'women's time' that is outside history and politics, or the circumscribed female-centred narrative of the woman who waits.[18] Instead, as Rowe Karlyn suggests, the film reimagines the temporal and spatial possibilities of cinematic narrative itself. Gorris, she writes, dispenses altogether with 'the cinematic rhythms and patterns of the Oedipal plot, with its linear, individually focused, conflict-ridden sense of time and its lone hero's drive to discover who he is through conquest, romantic or otherwise'. Instead, the film 'evokes another kind of time experienced in community rather than in the isolation of the individual body' (2011: 232–3). It is a re-vision, adds Rowe Karlyn, that involves a 'reimagining [of] time and space' (ibid.: 236).

Time

The narrative opens with a consideration of time. Over a shot of the old woman Antonia lying in bed the voice-over begins, 'Even before the sun had risen, Antonia knew her days were numbered. She knew more than that, she knew this would be her last day.' The voice-over distances us from Antonia, as does the framing of the single two-minute take which begins as a mirror shot and follows Antonia as she rises slowly from her bed, pauses before her mirror to adjust her hair, puts on her dressing gown, and then leaves the room. The camera moves fluidly with Antonia but maintains a distance throughout, and during the opening five-minute sequence we repeatedly see her within frames: those of her mirror, where she utters the only diegetic words of the sequence, 'Yes. It's time to die', and of the doors and windows through which we look first out at her as she opens the farmhouse shutters and feeds her goat, and then, finally, when she has returned once more to the house, in at her pensive face. This last shot, as she gazes out of the kitchen window, offers to draw us finally into her point of view, but the reverse shot that follows is a dissolve that takes us back in time, as a red bus moves past to block the camera and then reveal a much younger Antonia and her daughter Danielle standing in a village square, in 1940s dress and with suitcases in hand. 'Is this it?' asks Danielle as they slowly walk past the village café-bar whose wall carries British and American flags and an unevenly painted message: 'Welkom to our Liberaters'.

Time in this opening sequence is, then, complex and multiple. In the depiction of Antonia it moves slowly, Antonia's laboured, circular movements and the domestic detail rendering it, in Braidotti's words, both embodied and situated (Braidotti, in Butler 1994: 42). It is measured in both daily rhythms ('Even before the sun had risen') and generational lifespans, and in this respect it can be known, through lived experience and through memory. It can also be frozen in art – as it tracks to the window to observe Antonia, the camera shows us a series of portraits drawn in charcoal or chalk, of the film's characters as we will see them at different ages – or make sudden leaps. Yet if all this refuses the 'linear, individually focused, conflict-ridden sense of time' which Rowe Karlyn sees (2011: 233) as characterising the usual cinematic narrative, in this opening sequence historical time is not absent. We know that Antonia and Danielle arrive in the village at the end of World War II and that the village has been occupied and recently liberated. Later we will learn of its history of resistance and collaboration and of the shameful cowardice of its priest, who would not bury the villager shot for hiding a Jewish family. Whereas in *Broken Mirrors* the temporal rhythms of the women's lives interrupted and decentred the forward movement of the masculine narrative, however, here those rhythms dominate. The linear progression of history is present, but its markers remain at the periphery of the film's narrative space, registered largely through the visits to the city made first by Antonia and Danielle, in the search for a father for Danielle's child, and then by Thérèse as student and then lecturer. Only where it erupts as violence into Antonia's world (Pitte's rape of Deedee [Marina de Graaf] and Thérèse, Crooked Finger's [Mil Seghers] suicide) do we become aware of its ever-threatening power.

For Antonia's line, time is marked by seasons and generations, the rhythms of the body (Danielle's desire for a child; Antonia's renewed sexual desire 'after all these chaste years'; the births and deaths), and the repetitions and ebb and flow of community. It may be fecund ('Time gave birth again and again') or brutal (time 'tore through life like a vulture in search of prey'). This is not – or not always – suspended time in Baraitser's sense, but its flow is not the forward, teleological movement of history or of realist narrative: what Mary Ann Doane has called the 'unrelenting forward movement' (2002: 27) of mainstream cinematic narrative. Rather, it is seen as beyond the control of humanity and its cinematic expression is marked by interruptions, repetitions and moments of pause and stillness. It is interrupted, first, by fantasy, in the visions of painter Danielle which have inspired the identification of the film with magic realism,[19] and which provide a humorous but pointed rewriting of dominant cultural myths. The Christian story of resurrection is re-imagined in Danielle's vision of her foul-mouthed grandmother sitting up in her coffin, singing 'My Blue Heaven' to the accompaniment of priest and choirboys, and blessed by a smiling plaster Christ. Later, we share her visions of an avenging stone angel and a lesbian reworking of Botticelli's 'Birth of Venus'. It is a temporality marked by repetition in the frequent scenes whose choreographed rhythms punctuate a linear temporal flow, most notably those of Antonia the sower striding across the fields, of the visits to Crooked Finger of three generations of daughters, and those at the farm's welcoming courtyard table, with its shifting population of family and friends. In all of these, what we experience is time as continuity and duration, a series of presents that interact with both past and future. Finally, time is *stilled* in the many evocations of Dutch landscape painting whose temporal stasis and complex citational structure, as Geetha Ramanathan argues, both arrest and interrogate the film's temporal flow (2006: 181).

Mid way through the film, time is itself debated, in a discussion between the intellectually precocious child Thérèse and the nihilistic, reclusive philosopher Crooked Finger, whose response to the horrors of the twentieth century has been to embrace the pessimistic philosophy of Schopenhauer. 'But what about time?' asks Thérèse (Carolien Spoor); 'Did we invent time?' 'We made it up', responds Crooked Finger. In the dialogue that follows, the two play with the idea that different life forms might inhabit their own temporalities: 'Perhaps ants live in their time ... And crickets ... And trees ... And stars.' The linear time of history, it is suggested, is a construction; there are other modes of conceptualising and of living time. The exchange ends, however, with the child in the arms of the philosopher. 'Finger, you stink!' she exclaims, and he replies, 'That, my dear, is the smell of time past.' In these final words of the exchange we are returned to the embodied present, to the fact that our present bears corporeal traces of the past, and to the understanding that abstract concepts are always entangled with lived experience. It is Finger's failure to embrace this knowledge that leads to his philosophical nihilism and ultimately his suicide. Whilst it is tempting, then, to align Thérèse's comments with Kristeva's concept of 'women's time', it is not a separate time, monumental, cyclic and outside history and politics, that distinguishes Antonia's matriarchal 'line'. It is rather, as Lisa Baraitser (2017) suggests in her theorisations of time as care, a different way of living with and within time.

Space

Antonia 'carve[s] out a realm of freedom in a farm of her own', writes Karen Jaehne (1996: 28) in her review of the film. Like references to Kristeva's 'women's time', however, this invocation of Virginia Woolf, though it signals the film's feminism, does not capture the complexity of its reimagining of cinematic time and space. Antonia's space is not closed or private, a place away from the larger patriarchal world or the demands of the domestic. Indeed, for Geetha Ramanathan it is the framing of Antonia in landscape, 'so infrequent in mainstream film for women' (2006: 183), that prompts her characterisation of the film as feminist myth. But this is not landscape as backcloth for the hero's journey. Antonia's space is fluid and open, moving easily between inside and outside, as we saw in the opening sequence. It is a way of reimagining a living within space that has nothing to do with heroism ('carv[ing] out a realm') or conquest.

The village that we first meet is thoroughly patriarchal. But though small and apparently cut-off ('Is this it?'), its institutions echo those of the wider society, as we see not only through the history of war-time atrocities that Antonia tells but in the later ventures of Danielle and Thérèse into the city, where women are as marginalised and male arrogance as prominent as they are in the village. When the rapist Pitte returns, he returns in a soldier's uniform. All the public spaces of the village belong to men. Repeated high-angle shots emphasise the division in the church: men on one side of the aisle, women on the other, and the male priest (Leo Hogenboom) in his pulpit towering over the congregation in his celebration of men and denunciation of women. Farmer Daan (Jakob Beks) occupies the equivalent space in the all-male bar, boasting of his two sons 'ready to be put out to stud', and hauling his daughter before the assembled men to offer her to any prospective husband. 'The farmers here only breed sons,' says Antonia to Danielle. Outside, a public wall is 'the Saturday night urinal'; women are confined within walls and silence. Inside Farmer Daan's walled farmyard 'the men's loud voices [ride] roughshod over the women's silence', and women are abused and raped. This is a space of Freudian 'family secrets', but the incest that takes place is a matter of power, not desire. Antonia's mother, too, has been subject to such treatment, and dies consumed by rage and bitterness as a result. Once Antonia settles on the farm that she inherits, with its 'pink house', paths and fences mark the boundaries between her land and the men's spaces, and it is men who drive the tractors along the borders.

Positioned on the edge of the village, Antonia's farm might in another narrative be presented, like the brothel in *Broken Mirrors*, as an 'abject zone' (McClintock 1995: 72): marginalised, ignored and policed, its inhabitants society's outcasts. But whereas in *Broken Mirrors* this marginal space could be briefly recuperated, here its joyous habitation is the whole focus of the film. When mother and daughter enter the village for the funeral of Antonia's mother Allegonde, Antonia guides Danielle and the viewer past the various spaces which house the villagers, all fixed in their separation: Crooked Finger's house, Chiel the blacksmith's smithy, the rooms of Mad Madonna (Catherine ten Bruggencate) and the Protestant (Paul Kooij) separated by their institutional faiths. In contrast, Antonia's farm is marked by openness and a fluidity between interior and exterior: the most frequent scene is that of the courtyard table at which Antonia's extended family eats, talks, quarrels and dances. The wrought iron gates which mark the boundary of this space stand open.

Elsewhere, we see the family in the fields, haymaking and mending fences, as well as in the kitchen and bedroom. The women, says the narrator, 'had so little to do with the village that the villagers accepted them', but what the film shows us is a gradual reversal of this relationship between margin and centre: the villagers begin to congregate around the table, so that in the final iteration of the scene, all of them – living and dead, friend and enemy – are gathered there. Allegiances are reversed during the course of the film, so that when Antonia enters the village

Figure 2.3 The courtyard table

to confront the rapist Pitte, it is the young men who silently exact physical punishment on her behalf whilst she pronounces judgement, in a curse that echoes those of her mother at the beginning of the film but now carries a power previously absent.

Antonia's is, then, a utopian matriarchal space: what Rowe Karlyn calls a 'feminist democracy' (2011: 239). It can admit men provided that they do not assert dominance, as we see from the progress of Antonia's relationship with Farmer Bas (Jan Decleir). From his initial marriage proposal, which occurs – uncomfortably – in the doorway which marks the boundary of her space, to her initiation of a sexual relationship which must take place in a neutral space – 'not in my house or yours' – to their final dance around the communal table, we are presented with the spatial terms on which a successful heterosexual relationship may be negotiated. This, however, is not straightforwardly 'women's space' any more than it is 'women's time'. The film's repeated evocations of Dutch landscape painting not only have the effect of stilling time; they also remind us that this is a landscape that has already been mediated as well as occupied, and that even in this film that seeks to reimagine the temporal and spatial possibilities of cinematic narrative, a kind of generic 'overwriting' is necessary. As Antonia the sower strides across the field scattering seeds, we see a gendered reversal of Millet's 'The Sower' of 1850 and the 1888 version by Van Gogh which it inspired. Elsewhere, the haymaking scene and the framed landscapes cite those of seventeenth-century Dutch painters such as van Ruisdael (Jaehne 1996: 27–8), and interior shots echo Vermeer. Noting these references, Karen Jaehne sees the film, like the paintings it quotes, as seeking 'the conquest of the visible world' (ibid.: 27). The film's evident use of quotation, however, insists on the mediated nature of these landscape images. This is not a celebration of landscape as 'conquest' but rather a questioning of the terms on which landscape has been celebrated. Millet's social realist 'Sower' has been seen as a plea for social justice, but objectifies its central figure nonetheless. Gorris' film uses and reverses the symbolic features of such landscape painting (its Manichean images pit Antonia's sunlit farm against the dark menace of Farmer Daan's), whilst at the same time pointing to both the labour (we repeatedly see Danielle at work) and the (male) tradition involved in painting: in the glimpse we see of Danielle at art school she has to draw a version of Rodin's 'The Thinker'.

Community and subjectivity

In creating a continuum between the film's vision and the ironic, playful reversals of painter Danielle, whose imaginings encompass a lesbian reworking of Botticelli's 'Birth of Venus' and a matriarchal resurrection, these images also point us to another of the film's reworkings: that of an understanding of subjectivity as abstract and individual. The opening sequence begins, as we saw, with a female voice-over and a female protagonist. The relationship between the two, however, is complex. The third-person narrative voice is not that of Antonia, but it has access to Antonia's knowledge and memories; the dissolve that introduces Antonia's arrival in the village is signalled as flashback – Antonia's memory – but is introduced in the third person. It comes not when Antonia looks inward, at herself in the mirror, but when she gazes outwards. What the film gives us is a doubled point of origin and authority for its narrative, and this focal split, together with the film's visualisation of Danielle's fantasies and the many moments when its painterly images arrest narrative flow, give it a sense of multiple, polyvocal authorship and what Victoria Browne calls 'polytemporality': an internally complex, "composite" time, generated through the interweaving of different temporal layers and strands' (2014: 2). It is a polyvocality in which we, too, are implicated: as spectators we will have access to Danielle's transgressive imaginings, but Antonia will not. At the film's close the narrator, who has seemed omniscient, will herself be positioned within the narrative. 'And I, Sarah, her great-granddaughter, would not leave the deathbed of my beloved great-grandmother', she says, and we realise that this narrator is the Sarah whose childhood poems we have heard

Figure 2.4 Antonia and Sarah

and whose vision has introduced the final courtyard scene. Yet the Sarah we see is a child, and the voice is adult, so that we do not know the precise relationship between the two, or the temporal point of narration.

This is a narrative, then, with a collective protagonist, weaving together, as Rowe Karlyn writes, the voices and visions of five generations of women and the community they build 'around a concept of continuity that is based ... on female, generational lineage extending expansively through time' (2011: 232). The women of Antonia's line are distinct – a farmer, a painter, a mathematician and composer and a writer – but intimately, corporeally connected. They are daughters and mothers, but mother differently – Antonia is a single parent, Danielle has a lesbian partner, and Thérèse delegates the mothering role to her male partner – and share these roles with other women and some men. The film presents us with a model of subjectivity that is relational and embodied. Love is celebrated, most notably in the joyous montage of four varied couples engaged in sex, which builds to a glorious fanfare climax, but work and death, too, are shared bodily experiences, as are ideas – as we saw in the debate about time – and art.

That this is also a precarious community is clear from the outset. We do not know where Antonia and Danielle have come from at the start of the film,[20] but we repeatedly see the vulnerability of the community's members to the personal and institutional violence that threatens just beyond its borders. Deedee and Thérèse are raped, Loony Lips (Jan Steen) is subject to exploitation and ridicule, and Letta (Wimie Wilhelm) arrives at Antonia's gates with the words, 'I've nowhere else to go'. The community that is built from such origins suggests those described by Adriana Cavarero, for whom it is our vulnerability to others that connects us, and the mutual recognition which follows that permits self-realisation or 'self-narration'. For Cavarero, the creation of spaces for women that are 'shared, contextual, and relational' generates not only such mutual affirmation and authorisation but also a form of resistance that is 'clearly perceived and affirmed as political' (2000: 59–60). The communal space of Antonia's line is similarly political, despite the efforts of reviewers to insist on its 'lightheartedness'.

The film's final courtyard scene draws these threads together. It is prefaced by a voice-over reflection on time, which ignores 'all those things that are so important to us that we forget Time', as we watch with Antonia and her great-granddaughter Sarah as an old tree is cut down, a further death to add to those we have witnessed. The camera holds on their reflective faces in turn, so that the scene that follows is already doubly authorised. It is a return to the film's beginning, on the day of Antonia's death, and opens with a high angle view of the courtyard table and its occupants, with the following shot identifying this as the child Sarah's viewpoint as she gazes down from the hayloft where she sits with her notebook. A close-up of Antonia and Farmer Bas follows as they smile at one another, and then we see the arrival of Crooked Finger at the open gates. He smiles and beckons to Sarah as he did in life, and she responds. We then see Antonia's mother sitting in her coffin, and soon all the film's characters, alive or dead, friends or enemies, are present. As Antonia and Farmer Bas get up to dance, they are now decades younger, now once more old. Returning from the dance, Antonia prepares to leave the courtyard and the camera frames her alone, as she lifts her eyes to Sarah, beckoning her. Sarah returns her gaze.

In this final scene of community, then, temporalities, spaces and subjectivities are blurred. Time reverses, stills and accelerates, and Antonia's courtyard space now holds all the film's characters. Space and time, as Rowe Karlyn notes, 'have merged' (2011: 247). We see through the eyes of the child Sarah, but these are not her memories or her story. At the close of this narrative of a woman's life, there is no unified subject-identity to authorise and historicise her story, smoothing it into a linear whole. Instead, subjectivity is multiple and relational, shared between Antonia, the child Sarah and the voice-over which now resumes, repeating the words that began the film. As the narrator speaks, the camera circles slowly round the group assembled around Antonia's bed, as it circles so often in the film, capturing their touches and embraces. Once again, this is a relational consciousness: whilst Antonia's gaze moves across the faces of her family, her thoughts, and theirs, are voiced by the narrator but expressed visually on Antonia's face as she responds. When, therefore, the voice finally reveals itself to be that of the adult Sarah, not omniscient but located *within* the narrative world, the effect is to draw the spectator too into that world, positioning us, as does the circling camera, within this story of matrilineal resistance and continuity, and inviting us, since as the film's final written caption reminds us, 'nothing has come to an end', to continue it.

Embodied genealogies: what if . . .?

Antonia's Line is Marleen Gorris's most fully realised authorial vision. Whatever the difficulties in making it, unlike the films that were to follow it was, she writes, 'an author/director movie. I never had to make concessions, and when needed, I could change, rewrite and adapt as I went along. And I had the final cut' (2023). A 'bit of a myth', as she characterised it, the film refuses myth's heroic narrative, its fixed and self-enclosed quality, and its privileging of the 'hidden order' of things[21] revealed by its narrative (Ermarth 1998: 6). In its place it offers a 'story of lineage and descent' (Ramanathan 2006: 182) which is female, feminist and thoroughly embodied. Instead of a sovereign individual subject as hero, its subjects are embodied, relational and bound together by an ethics of care. Temporality is complex, overlapping, non-linear; it is marked by seasons and generations, the rhythms of the body and of community; it may be fecund or brutal. It flows beyond the control of humanity, but it is also interrupted, doubled and stilled. Space is fluid, expanding into landscape but not seeking to control it.

It is, many commentators have suggested, a utopian vision. Certainly it is as much a 'What if. . .' narrative as *The Last Island* or *A Question of Silence*. Yet Antonia's line is not outside history and linear temporality: both are there at the margins of the narrative, ever-present, threatening and powerful. In Antonia's space–time, however, the nascent, fragile and marginal communities of women pictured in Gorris's first two films and the half-suggested female genealogy glimpsed at the end of *The Last Island* are fully realised and celebrated, and the temporal and spatial possibilities of cinematic narrative reimagined.

Notes

1 The rights now lie with international media conglomerate CLT-UFA.

2 Personal communication from Nico Bruinsma, September 2023.

3 This is, for example, the grouping followed by Cult Epics, who released the three as a box set in 2023.

4 DuPlessis is here referencing Adrienne Rich's noted statement:

> Re-vision – the act of looking back, of seeing with fresh eyes, of entering an old text from a new critical direction – is for women more than a chapter in cultural history: it is an act of survival … We need to know the writing of the past, and know it differently than we have ever known it; not to pass on a tradition but to break its hold over us (Rich 1979: 35).

5 Overwriting because 'the original genre that is overwritten is still visible in its new format' (Ramanathan 2006: 177–8).

6 With the exception of Shakespeare, writes Volkmann, 'no other single literary work in the English language has received a similar amount of literary interest and scholarly research' (2011: 132). Jean-Jacques Rousseau was a notable early admirer, presenting it as the one book which the child Émile *must* read ([1762] 1974: 147).

7 The novel created its own literary genre of stories set on a desert island, the Robinsonade.

8 Another foundational text for this myth, *The Swiss Family Robinson*, originally published in 1812, is an exception in including the mother, but the omniscient father is the narrator, and the narrative follows his education of his four sons into manhood.

9 Kurtz's last words in *Heart of Darkness* are 'The horror! The horror!'. Marlow, the narrator, is able to draw back from the darkness that Kurtz sees because of his preoccupation with the practicalities of managing and mending the expedition's boat.

10 Samuel Taylor Coleridge, 'The Rime of the Ancient Mariner' Part II ([1798] 2000).

11 Nick's white ceremonial uniform is of a style discontinued in the 1970s.

12 In interview (Gorris 1990: 16), Gorris was clear that this, too, referenced the biblical 'If your hand causes you to sin, cut it off' (Mark 9:43).

13 *The Ship of Fools* is Sebastien Brant's fifteenth-century satire on governmental folly and corruption, possibly illustrated by Albrecht Dürer. Its most famous visual realisation is in the painting by Dutch painter Hieronymus Bosch (*c*. 1490–1500).

14 Gorris's screenplay, published in 1990, reads (p. 246):

> JOANNA
> (*after a slight pause, she says decidedly*)
> Yes. We'll finish the boat.
>
> She nods to herself and stares straight ahead with a slight smile on her face.
>
> Mrs Godame's quick glance at her passes unawares. The old woman looks worried and forlorn, far less assured than she had previously sounded. For one split second Mrs Godame's face is flooded with despair and doubt. Then her eyes return to the gently lapping waves.
>
> Joanna noticed nothing of this.
>
> Both women stare out across the sea.

15 See for example Maslin (1996), Thomas (1996), Levy (1996), Wilmington (1996), Bovkis (1997).

16 In her use of the Furies of Aeschylus in *A Question of Silence*, and in her use of both Christian mythology and the fairy tale in *Broken Mirrors*. See Chapter 1.

17 In a 1996 interview, Gorris commented on the film that 'I loved playing around with people's perceptions of things – like when Danielle wants a child, she's not going to look for a husband, she's going to look for somebody who can make her pregnant. That happens to be the knight on the white charger, and then they go to a castle, but the castle is a hotel' (Sklar 1996: 27).

18 As Teresa de Lauretis argues, this story 'like any other story, is a question of *his* desire' (1984: 133, italics added).

19 See in particular J'Nan Morse Sellery (2001), who argues that Danielle's 'magical' visions are one of the techniques that Gorris uses to disrupt the male gaze. See Ramanathan (2006: 180–1) for a rejection of this identification. Danielle's visions, she points out, are specific to her, and the film is concerned to authorise this vision rather than establish the magical as an ontological reality.

20 Asked about this in interview, Gorris responded that she left it 'to people's imagination. I thought maybe for the first three minutes they might wonder where Antonia and Danielle come from, but then hopefully if I do well, they will be submerged in the film and forget about it' (Sklar 1996: 28).

21 Ermarth writes of linear narrative as leading to a knowledge of the 'hidden order of things' which underlies the narrative's 'sequence of appearances' (1998: 64).

3

Revisioning the literary past

The Oscar success of *Antonia's Line* meant that Gorris's films had a new audience, and she was offered English-language films to direct. Financial constraints did not, however, disappear. Midway through shooting *Mrs Dalloway*, she reports, the British producer ran out of money and the production 'was put on hold for about two weeks, an American financing company and two new producers took over and we just managed to finish it' (Gorris 2023). The break in filming resulted in inevitable changes in crew midway through shooting (Palmer 1998). *The Luzhin Defence*, which followed, was given only limited release in both the UK and the US: the English producer, comments Gorris, didn't 'ma[k]e much of an effort', and 'Sony Classics in the States did not help it along much' (2023). These films nevertheless represented a significant shift for her: from low-budget, independent, 'authored' films into a mainstream genre, that of the literary adaptation or 'heritage' film. The move meant that she found herself having to defend the shift in tone from her earlier films; she seemed, insisted interviewer Augusta Palmer, 'much less angry' than before (Palmer 1998). It also brought a very different kind of review. Philip French, who had condemned *A Question of Silence* as 'intrinsically stupid' and 'reckless', 'as rigid in its thinking as any hard-line Stalinist movie' (1983: 30), now praised *The Luzhin Defence* as a 'work of considerable intellectual and physical elegance', noting in particular Emily Watson's 'radiant smile and blue eyes' (French 2000). Gorris herself insisted on the continuity between her films: 'I make the films that I want to make and the audience will see what they do' (Palmer 1998). All of her films, she has said, concern 'the survival of women in a patriarchal world' (Gorris 2023).

Mrs Dalloway (1997)

In *A Room of One's Own* Virginia Woolf writes: 'I tried to remember any case in the course of my reading where two women are represented as friends . . . . They are now and then mothers and daughters. But almost without exception they are shown in their relation to men' ([1929] 1993: 74–5). Woolf is writing of the difficulties women find in writing novels in the face of the 'fictitious woman' found in male-authored literature. Most women, she adds, have not written; instead, they 'have sat indoors all these millions of years, so that by this time the very walls are permeated by their creative force' (ibid.: 79). When they *have* presumed to write, their books have been deemed 'insignificant', for a 'scene in a battle-field is more important than a scene in a shop' (Ibid.: 67). Woolf's description of the woman whose creative intelligence is stifled by her confinement within the domestic, and whose life registers only 'in her relation to men', could refer to her own fictional creation, Clarissa Dalloway. Her summary of the critical evaluation of the work of the woman novelist is in part, of course, a reference to the reception of her own work.

Woolf's *Mrs Dalloway* takes place during a single day in June 1923. Clarissa Dalloway, middle-aged wife of a politician, prepares for the society party she will host that night at her London home. Her thoughts return to her youth in 1890 at her family's country house, Bourton, and her relationships with Sally Seton and Peter Walsh, whom she rejected in favour of Richard Dalloway. Visiting a florist's early in the day, Clarissa sees young war veteran, Septimus Warren Smith, who is suffering from delayed shellshock. Returning home, she receives Peter Walsh who has returned after years in India. Meanwhile, Septimus' wife Rezia takes him to see Sir William Bradshaw, a shell-shock specialist, because diagnosis by a general practitioner, Holmes ('nothing whatever the matter'), has been obtuse and dismissive. Bradshaw pronounces Septimus seriously ill, but later sends Holmes to institutionalise him, prompting Septimus to jump from a window to his death. At the party Clarissa greets her guests, who include the Prime Minister, as well as Peter and Sally, now wife of a mill-owner and mother of five. Bradshaw arrives late because of Septimus' suicide. Clarissa, repelled by Bradshaw's account of Septimus' death, retreats to a balcony, where she reflects on her fears of life and old age and admires Septimus' courage in choosing death. She returns to her party.

This is the territory that Marleen Gorris enters with her fifth film, an English-language adaptation of Woolf's novel, and in this and *The Luzhin Defence* (2000) which followed, adaptation of these early twentieth-century modernist texts is effected through engagement with the cinematic equivalent of one of Woolf's 'insignificant' fictional genres, the costume drama. Neither film was scripted by Gorris, and this move into the (feminised) mainstream which Michelle Citron, contemplating a similar move from 'film-maker to director', described as 'trading control for power'[1] (1988: 57) was productive of both surprise, in those critics who knew her earlier films and saw her as abandoning the 'ferocity' (Wilmington 1998) of their 'hard-edged feminism' (Sarris 1998), and evaluation in quite different terms.

To work within mainstream narrative film, adds Citron, is 'to work within a genre' (Citron 1988: 59) with all its attendant assumptions and constraints. Both *Mrs Dalloway* and *The Luzhin Defence* were seen as genre films, examples of the post-1980s 'heritage film' characterised by Christine Geraghty as 'based on literary sources and [telling] stories of upper-middle-class life in exquisite settings and with careful attention to the detail of costume and décor' (2008: 50). Female-focused, these 'up-market costume dramas' (ibid.: 54)[2] offered the visual pleasures of costume and setting, with a familiar, often romance-led narrative played out by a 'procession of . . . actors known for their theatrical credentials' (ibid.). Andrew Higson, the most influential writer on these films, sees them as 'turning their backs on the industrialized, chaotic present' of the 1980s to 'nostalgically reconstruct an imperialist and upper-class Britain' (1993: 110): a Britain of country houses, pastoral landscapes and interior design, in which political and social conflicts can be resolved within a liberal-humanist consensus (Higson 1996: 238–9) framed always by a nostalgic gaze. Higson groups Gorris's *Mrs Dalloway* with Merchant Ivory's *A Room with a View* (1986) as 'low-budget art-house oriented' versions of the heritage film characterised by a tone of 'polite decorum' (2003: 14). Some reviewers echoed this view, writing about the film as a 'fine period drama – humane, compassionate, perceptive' (Wilmington 1998), evoking 'a time when men walked the streets in top hats and wore fresh carnations in the buttonholes of their morning coats' (Ellis 1998), or, rather less positively, as 'a Merchant-Ivory quota quickie' (Sweet 1998: 6). It was noted that the film's key actors, Vanessa Redgrave and Rupert Graves, had both appeared in Merchant Ivory films: Redgrave in *Howards End* (1992) and Graves in *A Room with a View* (1985) and *Maurice* (1987). For Woolf scholar Leslie Kathleen Hankins, this generic positioning is a source of critical concern. 'Marleen Gorris's *Mrs. Dalloway*', she writes, 'is marketed . . . as a Merchant Ivory love story about courtship, chaste kisses, lost youth, old houses and dinner parties' (1999: 370); it replaces Woolf's radicalism with conventionality and her aesthetic experimentation with costume drama (ibid.: 373). Hankins' criticism is certainly true of the film's publicity poster that she highlights, in which, as she writes, 'young Richard kisses Clarissa as they stand on a primrose path up to a large country estate – a scene not even in the novel – while from a corner a benign older Clarissa looks on with a smile . . . Nostalgia and youth triumph' (ibid.: 369, 70). We might note, however, that a similar criticism might be levelled at the novel's own recent book covers which also feature flowers, aristocratic young women and society parties.

Hankins' parenthetic comment here indicates another major issue in the film's critical reception: the question of fidelity – or adequacy – to Woolf's vision. Reviewers familiar with the novel emphasised the difficulty of translating into film what Hankins calls its 'rich, dazzling surface . . . elastic and supple narrative play, and . . . complex, multifaceted cultural critique' (ibid.: 373). For some, like Janet Maslin and Andrew Sarris, Gorris's film succeeded, whilst for others it failed, reducing 'all that was mysterious or aching in the book to . . . trifling superficiality' (Keough 1998), or simply faced an impossible task. For David Denby, for example, Woolf's 'rich mental atmosphere – thick, bounding, grave yet playful – cannot be recaptured on film; anyone who tried it would simply get visual hash. The movie doesn't offer hash; it is well ordered, beautiful, and clear. But it does what movies do, not what Virginia Woolf does' (Denby 1998).

Where the film was seen as succeeding, its success was attributed less to the director, whose involvement in such a project was seen as puzzling or inappropriate ('Gorris seems . . . temperamentally unsuited to Woolf'[3]), than to scriptwriter Eileen Atkins, whose 'exquisitely constructed script' softens Gorris's 'feminist rigor' (Schwartzbaum 1998). Most of all, though, success was attributed to the film's star, Vanessa Redgrave, who was seen as 'authoring' the project. Redgrave, we learn, 'so loved the novel' (Ebert 1998) that she commissioned her friend Atkins to write the screenplay as a vehicle for herself (Wilmington 1998); Atkins then asked Gorris to direct. It is Redgrave who is seen as capturing the spirit of Woolf's novel: 'a majestic screen presence – so luminous and wise' (Guthmann 1998), she 'might well be the Platonic ideal of a Woolfish heroine' (Schwartzbaum 1998). Whilst for Hankins, then, the 'colour burning on a framework of steel' (1999: 368) which characterises Woolf's writing is missing in the film, for reviewer Andrew Sarris it is present, but produced not by the director but by the performance of its star. 'Ultimately', he writes, 'it is Ms. Redgrave who weaves all the tangled strands of the narrative into a tapestry of bright colors' (1998).

Figure 3.1 Vanessa Redgrave as Mrs Dalloway

Only Claire Monk in her review for *Sight and Sound* considers the film as 'Marleen Gorris' *Mrs Dalloway*' (1998: 53), despite the fact that Gorris herself saw the film in terms of her own vision and development: 'For me it was a sort of natural progression . . . I make the films that I want to make and the audience will see what they do', she said in response to the comment that, like *Antonia's Line*, it seemed 'much less angry' than her earlier films. The director as 'artist', she adds, needs 'the freedom of speech; the freedom to do what she or he wants to do' (Palmer 1998). She shot the film 'more or less as it was written', she later wrote, but did make changes in the editing (Gorris 2023). Here, I will consider the film in terms of this vision, and also of the constraints which this move into a mainstream 'feminine' genre both imposed and rendered visible.

'Marleen Gorris' *Mrs Dalloway*'

As Polina Rybina (2018) points out, we can track a number of visual and thematic continuities from Gorris's earlier films. Like *Antonia's Line* the film orders its flashbacks through window and mirror shots, and uses voice-over narration to introduce them. Like *Broken Mirrors* it defines femininity as performance, here in the form of Clarissa's party, and like both that film and *Antonia's Line* it uses dance to register sexual attraction. Septimus, who is driven to suicide by the horrors of war, recalls Crooked Finger in *Antonia's Line*. Both men choose death, as does Frank in *The Last Island*, in contrast to the women for whom, as Antonia says, 'life's got to be lived'. Finally, the kiss between the young Sally (Lena Headey) and young Clarissa (Natascha McElhone) is abruptly ended by unwanted male intrusion just as similar moments of lesbian intimacy are in both *Broken Mirrors* and *A Question of Silence*. Here, Peter's sardonic 'Star gazing?' which interrupts the moment underlines the impossibility of Clarissa's relationship with Sally and the freedoms it implies. As in the earlier films, however, the moment is held, disrupting both narrative progression in the flashback sequence and the clear separation of past and present.

It is with another echo that I want to begin, however. In one of the later scenes at Bourton, the young people go boating. As Peter (Alan Cox) rows the boat containing Dalloway (Robert Portal) and Clarissa, she begins to sing. In Woolf's novel the scene is filtered through Peter's memories, and recorded merely as 'she laughed; she sang' (Woolf [1925] 1992: 68). In the film, however, the young Clarissa wistfully sings the sea shanty, 'Away for Rio', as she gazes skywards. The soft focus and the stillness and length of the scene seem to abstract it from time and place. As the film cuts to the older Clarissa (Vanessa Redgrave) twirling before her mirror with the dress she will wear to her party, the song continues softly. Like the 'star gazing' kiss, this scene seems to point beyond the closed worlds of Bourton and Clarissa's later London home to the possibility of other lives and relationships. At the same time, however, these stiffly posed figures in their formal evening clothes, bound together in a circular journey with no outcome, recall the similarly posed doomed figures in the ghostly boat of *The Last Island*. No less bounded than the deserted island of that film, Clarissa's worlds of country house and London society permit only glimpses of those moments of connection which in

Gorris's earlier films arrested narrative time and disturbed the concreteness of place.

Mrs Dalloway, then, no less than Gorris's earlier films, is concerned with how women survive in a patriarchal world. Like *Antonia's Line* it depicts survival in a post-war world in which war and patriarchy are indissolubly linked, but here that world is oppressively central and the woman within it isolated. The film departs from Woolf's novel in prefacing our introduction to Clarissa with a scene in the trenches, in which we view Septimus (Rupert Graves) framed by barbed wire as he gestures desperately towards the camera to the unseen Evans: 'Evans, don't come!' An explosion follows. For Hankins, this change 'undermines the design of Woolf's feminist insight' (1999: 369) since it foregrounds a battle scene ('a scene in a battle-field is more important than a scene in a shop'), but it provides a preface to the London of 1923 which we see next. Here, the signs of an oppressive patriarchal power are ubiquitous, from the monumental buildings whose phallic proportions are highlighted by the camera's low-angle pans, to the chimes of Big Ben which dictate the day, and the tall iron spikes and railings that repeatedly block our view of Clarissa's progress through the streets. Her street walking, though at times joyous ('What a lark! What a plunge!'), is both circular and rigidly bounded. When in the florist's shop she glimpses Septimus through the window, his face is bordered by an arrangement of flowers that echoes the shape of the barbed wire we saw earlier. This framing is then repeated in the reverse shot of Clarissa. Throughout, the two are similarly framed in mirrors and windows, and similarly trapped and menaced by the spikes and railings of London's streets.

If the film makes us constantly aware of the recent war, however, it also makes it clear that England's governing classes have learned nothing from it. Its pompous patriarchs still stroll to their weighty meetings and make judgments on the poor and powerless behind closed doors, while around them the streets are haunted by the presence of maimed ex-soldiers in ragged uniforms. As Richard Dalloway (John Standing) and Hugh Whitbread (Oliver Ford Davies) stand at the window of an arcade jewellers, musing on the relative value of jewellery and flowers as presents for their wives, a ragged ex-soldier, to them invisible, walks slowly past, bisecting our view of the two men; as Richard buys the promised flowers and walks happily towards the camera, another, blind and begging, sits behind him, occupying half of the frame. Clarissa herself, despite the parallels that the film draws, which echo Woolf's own observation that 'the public and the private worlds are inseparably connected ... the tyrannies and servilities of the one are the tyrannies and servilities of the other' ([1938] 1993: 270), remains equally oblivious. As she emerges onto a wide street on her way to the florist's she fails to see the disabled ex-soldier who crosses behind her. The camera, however, remains on him as she moves out of frame, and notes that another passer-by, much less well-dressed than Clarissa, does see and greet him.

The film, then, places Clarissa much more securely within a concrete historical world than does Woolf's novel, as reviewers noted, often critically. It seems, writes Hankins, 'rooted to the ground', without the dizzying temporal and spatial mobility of the novel's blurring of focalisation, perception and memory (1999: 371). Both the scene in the trenches and the day in London are dated, the latter precisely. Whilst the frequent temporal shifts to the Bourton of the 1890s produce breaks in the precise clock time that dominates Clarissa's day, they do not, like the flashbacks in *A Question of Silence*, give access to an expanded and other sense of place and temporality. The pre-war world of Bourton is as solidly present and fixed in time as the London of 1923. It is also irretrievably gone, cut off from the world of the 1920s by the war that divides them, a fact emphasised by the use of different film stocks, with the more richly coloured Kodak film used for the pre-war sequences (Higgins and Leps 2000: 121). The effect of the rapid and unmarked intercutting of the two worlds with their different groups of actors, very different from the long flashback in *Antonia's Line* with its emphasis on continuity, is thus to create a sense of doubled, concrete, but historically disconnected worlds, two cinematic presents in which 'a loss ... of connecting links' (Cuddy-Keane 1998: 173) means both separation and a constant re-echoing, a circular and entrapping repetition.

Both worlds are steeped in patriarchal power. Bourton is the possession of Clarissa's father and by 1923 has passed to her brother. Its men lead their lives largely elsewhere and its conventions are those of the Victorian double standard. When at the start of the film the older Clarissa opens her front door to the sounds of the London streets and her words 'What a lark! What a plunge!' dissolve into the same words spoken by the young Clarissa as she flings open the terrace doors at Bourton and runs across its formal gardens, we are struck first by the contrast. The older Clarissa's world is safe and ordered, and her voice-over words, 'It's so very dangerous to live for only one day', seem out of place in the affluent town-house through which we follow her, but more appropriate to the impulsive energy of the young Clarissa, who later echoes them. Yet the world of Bourton is equally enclosed. Although we constantly see the young Clarissa in motion, her running figure remains contained within the house and walled gardens of Bourton. There is no outside to escape to; her energy is an energy without outcome. When she and Sally discuss their dreams of the future ('We'll do everything together. We'll change the world!'), their dreams are bounded both spatially, by the world of Bourton, and temporally. They are bounded, too, by the conditions of social intelligibility: 'Marriage is a catastrophe for women,' says Sally; 'But it is inevitable, isn't it', adds Clarissa.

Another story?

Mrs Dalloway, commented reviewers, 'is a woman who will always wonder what might have been' (Ebert 1998). The film makes clear, however, not only that the freedom apparently offered by the young Peter ('You could do so much, *be* so much') is illusory, since he desires control, but that that represented by her relationship with Sally is unthinkable within this context. The world of Bourton *produces* the London of 1923, and the pre-war Clarissa, for all her innocence and moments of rebellion, is, like her older counterpart, both a trapped and a complicit figure. Her choice of Dalloway, who Peter says, 'will pamper you and keep you in a perfectly beautiful, safe prison', is the choice, she says, of 'room, room to breathe'. Yet as we follow the older Clarissa through London's streets and the public spaces of the Dalloway house with their polished silverware and rich furnishings, to ascend a narrow staircase to her garret room, she reflects on what this 'room' has become. As it was in the street, our view of her is constricted, this time by the huge balustrade which occupies half the frame, and her voice-over expresses this diminution. No longer 'Clarissa ... Just Mrs. Dalloway, Mrs. Richard Dalloway who's to give a party', she is now left to 'sleep undisturbed' while others are 'blackberrying in the sun'. Her small single room with its 'sheets stretched and ... bed narrow' signals that 'It's all over for me'. The space sought and gained, as Jane Marcus suggests of Woolf's own desire for a 'room of one's own', was merely that of 'privacy in confinement ... not to stretch into space without boundaries' (1994: 185).

In *Antonia's Line* the party which concludes the film is, like the film's relationships, expansive: Antonia's courtyard space now holds all the film's characters, living and dead, and the subjectivity through which it is visualised is multiple and relational. In *Mrs Dalloway*, Clarissa speaks of her desire to 'give people one night in which everything seems enchanted', from which they will 'go home thinking "Oh what fun it was! How good it is to be alive!"', and as in *Antonia's Line* this party concludes the film. The recipients of Clarissa's gift, however, members of the past and present ruling class, are ill equipped to appreciate it. The men are pompous, hypocritical and self-satisfied: politicians, as Richard patiently explains to Sir William Bradshaw, 'are not really very interested in shell-shock', or in any other post-war social issue. The women are self-effacing and fearful, like the unmarried Ellie Henderson (Kate Binchy), or forceful and manipulative, like Lady

Bruton (Margaret Tyzack), who plans to send all unemployed war veterans to Canada but needs the help of male politicians to achieve it. The narratives of gender and genre, public and private worlds, remain firmly in place. Clarissa herself, as Sally (Sarah Badel) points out, gives 'a performance' – one that is at once licensed, as the correct behaviour of a political wife, and desperately anxious: 'It's a disaster, the party's a disaster! I'm humiliated.' Her voice-over comments, so different from her spoken greetings, mark her self-absorption and isolation from her guests. When at the end of the film she returns to the party after her reflections on Septimus's death, to greet Peter (Michael Kitchen) with 'Here I am at last', the self she offers seems no less performed and isolated than before.

In Gorris's earlier films, as we saw, resistance and the glimpsed possibility of another story, lived or fantasised, were realised through the disruption of linear narrative in moments of suspended time and female connection, and sometimes in hal-lucinatory sequences. Here, such moments occur most vividly in the Bourton scenes: in the moments of physical intimacy between Sally and Clarissa which culminate in the suspended temporality of the kiss, with its suggested awakening of both passion and possibility; and in the boating scene, whose wistful conjuring of an imagined elsewhere suggests that this possibility is already attenuated. In the London of 1923 such narrative pauses recur, but they are no longer 'star gazing' moments (the older Clarissa gazes at a sky now inscribed with an advertising slogan written in smoke by an aeroplane). Instead, they are moments of horror and fear – Septimus's flashbacks to his wartime experience and Clarissa's vision of the faces and voices of the Bradshaws (Robert Hardy and Richenda Carey) as monstrous and distorted, as they speak of Septimus's death – or of memory and introspection cir-cumscribed by mirrors or windows. Peering tentatively through her curtains after her early walk to buy flowers, Clarissa sees Septimus once more, shocked and afraid, as he appeared before her through the window of the flower shop. The vision fades, however, to the ambiguously comforting words of Shakespeare's

'Fear no more the heat of the day', and Clarissa closes the curtains and returns to her mirror and her memories.

Later, when she withdraws from the party after her encounter with the Bradshaws, Clarissa retreats again to a window, this time opening it fully and stepping out onto the balcony. As she reflects on Septimus's death – 'There he lay with a thud, thud, thud in his brain and then a suffocation of blackness' – this time it is not Septimus that she sees but the spiked railings that signify her own entrapment as well as his death. Conceived of by Woolf as Clarissa's 'double' (Showalter 1992: xxvii) in the public, masculine world, the male figure who chooses death over life, the Septimus of the novel has been seen by critics both as a figure who demonstrates Clarissa's intuitive understanding of those very different from herself (Ingersoll 2017: 99), and as evidence that this empathy remains abstract, without any real human connection (Bell 2006: 96) . Here, Clarissa's focus on the threatening spiked railings suggests that Septimus remains a symbol to her; it is the contrasting pull in her own life between danger – we see again the moment of the kiss – and safety that absorbs her. Although she, like Antonia and Mrs Gadame in Gorris's earlier films, chooses 'life, to be lived, right through to the end', it is still safety that she values: 'Without Richard sitting there calmly reading the Times, while I crouched like a bird and gradually revived, I might have perished'.[4] Her final reflections, on those moments of 'immeasurable delight' that 'surprise us', stilling time so that 'you want to say to each moment "Stay! Stay! Stay!"', once more provide the glimpsed possibility of other temporalities and relationships. Spoken over the exchange of looks and smiles between Clarissa and the woman she now sees in the window opposite, they also recall the moments with Sally. It is an exchange of looks not in the novel, where Clarissa merely watches the old woman prepare for bed, but it remains an exchange across distance: the woman is framed like a painting within the grid of her Georgian window, unreachable, and after the exchange of looks she, like Clarissa, turns inside once more.

Time and place

Writing of the film's realisation of the kiss between Clarissa and Sally, Earl G. Ingersoll describes it as an 'evanescent Woolfian "moment"' (2017: 91). The argument that through the fluidity of its rendering of time and consciousness, Woolf's novel sought to challenge the dominance of linear 'clock time', represented in both novel and film by the 'irrevocable' chiming of Big Ben (Woolf [1925] 1992: 128), is one often made. James Miracky, for example, terms this public, linear time 'diachronic or external time', a temporality which is disrupted in the novel by 'synchronic' time: 'moments' that are both extended and fleeting, and which may also function as 'points of psychic convergence' for characters (2001: 226). For Lesley Higgins and Marie-Christine Leps this means that the novel counters the idea 'that life is individual, substantial and knowable', to insist on a subjectivity that is 'social, relational and constructed' (2000: 117), an idea that is very close to the sense of subjectivity that I have suggested can be found in the earlier films of Gorris. Yet, as reviewers noted, Gorris did not seek to render the shifting consciousness of the novel, instead rooting her characters in a strong sense of place and time, a fact that puzzled some reviewers and angered others. The reason, I think, lies in crucial differences between the two visions. For Gorris the power of social and political structures, always there in Woolf's work but not the foreground of her novels, is central, and limiting. Resistance means the disruption of these structures through embodied connection, so that in the moments of suspension of linear narrative another kind of temporality experienced in community becomes possible. The fluidity of consciousness of Woolf's characters, however, is always individual, occasionally coinciding but never quite meeting or joining. The film shows the limitations of these individualised moments against the power of social structures, their possibilities for connection only fleetingly glimpsed and quickly reabsorbed, as in Clarissa's contemplation of Septimus's death, into self-preoccupation and the comforts of social intelligibility that come with the expected narratives of class and femininity.

A double incarnation

For many reviewers it was Vanessa Redgrave as Clarissa who embodied the spirit of Woolf's novel, weaving 'all the tangled strands of the narrative into a tapestry of bright colors' (Sarris 1998). Less Mrs Dalloway than Woolf herself, Redgrave is a 'double incarnation. She is Mrs. Dalloway and she is Woolf, a gallant icon of a gracefully collapsing world' (Kroll 1998: 80). It is this 'cinematic misreading' that so angered Hankins, reducing the Woolf who was 'an experimental visionary artist, a feminist and social activist' to 'a society hostess' (1999: 372–3). This ambiguous identification, however, is I think crucial to the meaning of the film. In placing Clarissa so firmly within her historical world Gorris makes visible both its relentlessly suffocating structures and its seductions. Woolf's Clarissa is herself an ambiguous figure, at once society hostess whose concerns are 'trivial' (Showalter 1992: xliv) and recipient of Woolf's own reflections on life, loss and death (Rose 1986: 128). Redgrave's blurring of the two places Woolf, too, within her character's historical context – we, unlike Clarissa and Woolf, know what the complacency of the 1920s will produce – and reveals the ambiguities of her position.

Jane Marcus has written of the 'vacillation between safety and danger' (1994: 182) that characterises Woolf's writing. Her outsider status, suggests Marcus, was always compromised, product of a privilege that remained seductive. Woolf's 'room of one's own', she argues, is a space within, one bought and maintained by the 'blood money' of empire. It offered Woolf the freedom to write, and sanctuary, but its boundaries were also boundaries to the imagination, and its safety could be a form of imprisonment (ibid.: 185). Clarissa, the woman who does not write, reflects on that imprisonment, an imprisonment rendered visually acute in Gorris's film, but, like the other major characters (Sally has married for wealth and Peter has accepted his imperial role in India, casually commenting on 'coolies beat[ing] their wives'), she is seduced by the privilege of which she is part. In historicising Woolf through the doubly signifying figure of Redgrave, the film registers Woolf's own ambivalent position – a position she herself acknowledged[5] – as both critical feminist and privileged inheritor of the spoils of empire. Her individualised 'politics of trespass' (Marcus 1994: 173), manifested in Clarissa's brief moments of transgression and subsequently internalised as reflection, not action, are not enough. It may also, perhaps, speak to the position of its director, now also a woman who does not write and whose vision of other possibilities and temporalities can find only moments of expression against the seductions of the heritage film.

'Women's culture'

The 'two clarifying institutions of social intelligibility [are] genre and gender', writes Lauren Berlant (2011a: 176). In *The Female Complaint* (2008) she describes 'women's texts' as 'gendering machines' which offer 'modes of feminine sentimental fantasy' (2008: 35). This is largely how Gorris's *Mrs Dalloway* was received: as a low-budget, female-oriented costume drama whose flashback structure builds a 'nostalgic perspective ... into the narrative itself' (Higson 2003: 83). Only Roger Ebert recognised the film's emphasis on entrapment, suggesting that Clarissa is 'like a caged animal – trained, but not tamed' (1998). The film's ending seemed to reinforce this sense of nostalgia in the way that Higson suggests. Clarissa's reflections at the window are intercut with the reminiscences of Peter and Sally, and the film closes on a freeze-frame of the young Clarissa, Sally and Peter sitting at a tea table on the lawns of Bourton, in the moments before Clarissa tells Peter she will accept Dalloway's proposal. For Higgins and Lep, this is a nostalgic vision of the three young people 'enjoying the leisure of a privileged youth' (2000: 123), but the figures are separate and isolated, with both Clarissa and Peter looking away and down. Very different from the freeze-frame which closes *A Question of Silence*, where Janine is caught in the action of turning towards the group of women witnesses, this shot seems to emphasise the stasis and isolation of these figures: the very image of the costume drama, with its sumptuous clothing, elaborate social rituals and country house setting, it points also to its narrowness and sterility.

Gorris's first foray into the 'women's genre' of the costume drama is also an exploration of Woolf's response to the patriarchal capitalist world of her time, and it is the limitations more than the courage of that response that are emphasised. 'The circularity of the feminine project will not escape you', writes Berlant (2008: 20). The young Clarissa ends in the costume in which we first saw her, but her movement is now stilled, containing within the film's circular arc all the moments of protest and transgression that we have seen. Woolf's 'room of one's own' is, the film suggests, Clarissa's 'perfectly beautiful, safe prison' with its pleasures of normative femininity. Only at key moments is this circular narrative arrested and the possibility of another story,

Figure 3.2 *Mrs Dalloway*: ending

of vulnerability and connection, suggested. As viewers we are offered the 'feminine' cinematic pleasures of costume and setting, but we are also reminded that they are compromised pleasures and invited, though only momentarily, to look beyond.

The Luzhin Defence (2000)

The Luzhin Defence, Gorris's second adaptation of a critically celebrated modernist text, was reviewed, like *Mrs Dalloway*, in two ways: in terms of its adequacy to the vision of the author of its source text, and as an example of the 'heritage film'. In the first case, as in the review by Alan A. Stone, the tone was often dismissive. 'Far from capturing the novel's intellectual vigor', writes Stone, '[t]he film serves up a sugarcoated confection that will make anyone with a taste for Nabokov gag . . . . I can think of [no film adaptation] that is more disrespectful to the spirit of its author' (Stone 2001). In reviews of this kind, much of the review is devoted to demonstrating the reviewer's superior knowledge of Nabokov's novel and themes – or in some cases of the game of chess, the novel's subject matter. In the second case, the film was praised for the 'striking visual beauty' (Blackwelder 2001) of its settings and costumes, the 'fluidity and ease' of its 'beautifully accomplished cinematography'[6] (Scott 2001, Osborne 2001), its romantic, elegiac quality ('the movie has the dreamy quality of a lost world', Hunter 2001), and the excellence of its two principal actors, John Turturro and Emily Watson.

The language of the first group bristles with a defensive anger. Both Stone and Tim Krabbé, a chess specialist, accuse Gorris of 'disrespect', whilst Jonathan Rosenbaum (2001) writes of the film's 'distortions'; all identify this insubordination with Gorris's feminism. Krabbé writes that she has turned 'a novel about the tragic enchantment of chess into a feminist pamphlet' (Krabbé 2001); Stone opens by noting pointedly that the film premiered at the Boston Women's International Film Festival before referring more explicitly to Gorris's feminism, whilst Rosenbaum describes Gorris as 'a Dutch filmmaker who apparently wants to be known now for tangling with classy literary material' instead of sticking with the 'scary feminist rage' of her early films (Rosenbaum 2001). Both Stone and Bill Gallo of the *New Times* refer to Nabokov's novel as 'the real thing': 'ecstatic' (Stone 2001) and 'transcendent' (Gallo 2001). Gorris is seen to have debased this transcendent real, to such an extent that her film invites physical expulsion (it makes 'anyone with a taste for Nabokov gag', Stone 2001).

'[M]ost writing on adaptation as translation', comments James Naremore, 'cannot avoid a gendered language associated with the notion of "fidelity"' (2000: 8). But if this first group of reviews seems set on establishing the superiority of both Nabokov and the male reviewer, the praise of the second group is no less gendered. Here, however, Gorris is seen to conform to the expectations of the 'feminine' genre of the heritage film, supplying the visual pleasures and romance narrative required of a successful example. These are pleasures, however, that are firmly positioned within the hierarchy of artistic forms, as Stone makes clear in his final comment on the film. Gorris, he writes, 'has made a cinemato-graphically beautiful film empty of Nabokov's ecstatic genius' (2001). It is a hierarchy with a long history, as W. J. T. Mitchell makes clear in his analysis of Lessing's *Laocoon* of 1766.[7] Lessing, like his contemporary Burke, writes Mitchell, identifies painting, the visually beautiful, external display of bodies and spaces, with the feminine, whilst masculinity is identified with words, the intellect and the sublime (1984: 109). In very similar vein, Gorris's reviewers here celebrate Nabokov as 'the 20th century's greatest sorcerer in prose' (Poole 2000), 'the master of parody and pathos' (Stone 2001), whose intellectual vigour is manifest in his complex chess analogies but whose reflexive prose can also convey the transcendent. The visual beauty of Gorris's film, however, is external and superficial, a 'Merchant-Ivory gloss' (Rosenbaum 2001). Whereas Virginia Woolf's genius had to be defended against identification with Gorris's Mrs Dalloway, then, that of Nabokov is self-evident, 'the real thing' (Gallo 2001).

Nabokov's novel was published in Russian in 1930 and translated into English as *The Defense* in 1964. It follows Luzhin's development from unattractive, withdrawn child to shambling, eccentric adult, largely from within his consciousness. Luzhin retreats from family and school into chess and, mentored and exploited by Valentinov, who discards him when he ceases to be a boy prodigy, becomes a grandmaster. During a tournament at a resort he meets a young girl, proposes, and is accepted. Playing against Italian grandmaster Turati, he has a breakdown and is persuaded by his psychiatrist and fiancée to give up chess. He marries, but deprived of his profession Luzhin now begins to see his life as a chess game. Encounters with figures from his past, including Valentinov, persistently draw him back to chess and to 'that same passion which would destroy the dream of life' ([1964] 1994: 172). Concluding that the 'only way out' is 'to drop out of the game' (ibid.: 176), he climbs out of the bathroom window of his fifth floor apartment and, we assume, falls to his death.

Chess, as many critics have pointed out, was a recurring pre-occupation for Nabokov, himself a composer of chess problems who saw chess as 'a form of high art' (Alexandrov 1991: 58). For some critics, then, Luzhin's absorption in its patterns, frequently described in the novel in terms of music, represents a form of transcendence, a 'means of escape from the prism of temporally bound existence' (Alexandrov 1991: 66), whilst for others the intellectual abstractions of chess render it sterile, a symbol for 'all the patterns and systems that prove tragically inadequate when preferred to or violently superimposed on the natural flow of life' (Toker 2016: 67). In both cases *The Defense* is seen as a novel which centres on Luzhin's tragic inability to reconcile art/chess and life. This tragic conflict between 'matter and spirit' (Alexandrov 1991: 58) is a wholly masculine affair. Women in Nabokov's fiction, writes Elena Rakhimova-Sommers, may be either seductive and predatory or the male protagonist's 'intellectual and emotional bodyguard', in which case they are 'anemic [and] bodiless' (2017: xviii–xix). In both instances the woman functions only in relation to the male protagonist. In *The Defense* Luzhin's wife is never given a name; a featureless woman, she might be compared, writes Brian Boyd, to 'Woolf's Angel in the House' (1987: 595). For Nabokov himself, writing in the Foreword to the English language translation of 1964, she is merely 'a gentle young lady ... a dear girl', there to evidence a quality in Luzhin 'that transcends both the coarseness of his grey flesh and the sterility of his recondite genius' ([1964] 1994: ix). Though she tries to 'defend' him from chess, she fails to understand or to love Luzhin. His suicide, where he sees spread out below him a 'chasm' divided like a chessboard 'into dark and pale squares' ([1964] 1994: 178), signals for some critics his ultimate failure to reconcile 'human commitments and intellectual pursuits' (Toker 2016: 80); for others it represents Luzhin's final escape into 'the transcendent dimension of his world' (Alexandrov 1991: 68).

After a story by Nabokov

> 'I said yes to the original script of *The Luzhin Defence,*'based on' Nabokov's story. The film I delivered ended up rather more of an 'after a story by Nabokov' (Gorris 2023).

Scripted by Peter Berry, *The Luzhin Defence* is Gorris's sole film with a male protagonist. As hostile reviewers noted, however, this is only apparently the case, since Luzhin's fiancée (Emily Watson) is here given not only a name, Natalia Kharkov, but, as Ewa Mazierska suggests, the perspective through which we view Luzhin's story. Gorris, she writes, 'forces us to trust Natalia's judgement rather than Nabokov's' (2011: 153). It is, however, the only film by Gorris in which close relationships between women are absent, replaced by a feminised heterosexual relationship whose adequacy as resistance to the masculine structures in and against which it develops the film is concerned to examine. The key events of the novel are retained, but compressed into the period between Luzhin's first meeting with Natalia and their marriage, so that he dies before the wedding can take place, and – apart from flashbacks to Luzhin's childhood – into a single location, here an

Figure 3.3 *The Luzhin Defence*: ending

Italian lakeside hotel rather than the Berlin of Nabokov's novel. Gorris also adds a final sequence. After Luzhin's death Natalia completes the suspended match with Turati (Fabio Sartor) for the world championship, with the aid of a note providing the winning moves which Luzhin scribbled before his death. The film closes on her smiling face as, leaving the tournament building, she is filmed in slow motion walking confidently towards the camera, her gaze directed out beyond the frame.

If Luzhin (John Turturro) is Gorris's first and only male protagonist, he has clear antecedents in her films, from the powerless and unseen André in *Broken Mirrors* to Crooked Finger in *Antonia's Line* and Septimus in *Mrs Dalloway*. All are reclusive figures who have responded to the brutality of dominant power structures by immersing themselves in abstract systems and neglecting the body. Haunted by past trauma, all withdraw to the comfort of confined and airless spaces. We do not learn André's fate, but Luzhin's suicide echoes those of the isolated male figures in Gorris's two previous films. Like them Luzhin, as Mazierski writes (2011: 150), 'struggle[s] with physical space': he walks unsteadily, and away from the chess board is lost. Kidnapped and deposited in the countryside on Valentinov's (Stuart Wilson) orders, his disorientation is captured in a montage of low angle shots of an endless, featureless landscape into which he can only collapse. Unlike in Nabokov's novel, his immersion in chess does not bring timelessness and transcendence. Instead, the patterns of the chess board replicate in abstract form the patterned structures at work elsewhere in the film. As in *Mrs Dalloway* Gorris uses the visual patterns and social rituals of the heritage film to emphasise restriction. Uniform[ed] male figures dominate its spaces, from the regimented structures of the chess tournament, with its ranks of male competitors and audience, to the interchangeable chess officials in their morning suits, the brass band and line of uniformed hotel staff that greet Luzhin and Turati, and, less overtly visible but always present in the crowd scenes, the uniformed soldiers of Mussolini's fascist Italy. It is four of these soldiers who rescue Luzhin from his abandonment in the countryside; as they approach on a motorcycle we see that they are practising a parade manoeuvre.

For Nabokov, writes Vladimir Alexandrov, 'immersion in chess, like the experience of cosmic synchronization and writing poetry, stops time' (1991: 66). In Gorris's film, however, the escape into abstraction it offers both replicates and services the social and political world beyond it. Luzhin's childhood mastery of chess is played out in the gambling halls of St. Petersburg and then the salons and bars of interwar Europe, always for money. The lavishly orchestrated tournament of the film's present is for the entertainment of a moneyed elite thoroughly at home in fascist Italy – we hear Natalia's mother (Geraldine James) complaining of 'a Jewish conspiracy'. The chess tournament itself is an aggressively discordant contest, dominated by the ticking of chess clocks and the forceful striking of their stop mechanisms by the competitors as they slam down their pieces. Luzhin's introduction to it by his father (Mark Tandy) is as a duel: 'As Pushkin's doomed duellist said, 'Let's start, if you're willing'. Later, as he begins to see his life as a chess pattern, it is the domination of time that he reiterates: 'I must keep track of every second. Every second I must keep track of. Every second'. Chess is here characterised not by the timelessness of poetry or music but by the imprisoning narrowness of a heightened 'clock-time', and Luzhin is undone not by the intrusion of 'temporally bound earthly life' (Alexandrov 1991: 66) but by the dominance and exploitation of a succession of patriarchal figures (his father and 'chess father' Valentinov) and his own inability to embrace the fluidity of life.

'The only dance we dance'

Introducing Luzhin to chess, his young aunt (Orla Brady), his father's lover, says, 'This is your king, the most important piece on the board, and he knows it. But his moves are limited. . . . The queen, she's more agile. She's brave, and she's cunning, and she can move as far as she likes'. It is a speech not in Nabokov's novel, where the aunt introduces the chess pieces as participants in a royal battlefield ('King and Queen next to each other', then Officers, Horses and Cannons), though there too the introduction is tinged with sexual excitement (Nabokov [1964] 1994: 23). The aunt of Nabokov's novel is a seductive and elusive figure who betrays Luzhin to his father. In Gorris's film she is a mobile and energetic young woman who introduces him to the visceral excitement of a fairground rollercoaster ride and is more interested in the gendered symbolism of the chess pieces she names for him than in the game itself. When he encounters Natalia – as in the novel they meet when she returns to him items that he has failed to notice falling from his pocket – it is the echo of his aunt to which he is attracted. Natalia's red dress, worn only on this occasion in the film, recalls that worn by his aunt, and Natalia returns to Luzhin the glass chess king which he has dropped and which she will later say is 'so much a part of you'. It is, he mutters, 'Patterns repeating themselves'.

The film makes clear, however, that this is Luzhin's perspective, and its limitations are evident from the film's opening. The credit sequence begins with a black screen and the sound of a train. We are in a tunnel; ahead is a small patch of light with tracks leading toward and through it, and in the distance a second tunnel. As we approach it, the words 'Based on the novel by Vladimir Nabokov' appear on the black screen, and the sounds of the train grow louder. The film cuts briefly to a close-up of Luzhin's hands against the dark interior of the carriage, opening a tattered notebook crammed with chess notations, before it cuts to our first view of Natalia as she emerges from the shadow of a doorway into the space and light of the station platform. Against the black and white pattern of receding tunnels is set the light and colour of Natalia's entrance; against the dimly lit close-ups of Luzhin's hands, cigarette, chessboard and notebook[8] is set the openness of her slow, confident walk across the platform, through the massed uniforms of brass band, chess officials and soldiers, registering everything with an expression of amused expectancy. As Mazierska notes, 'she is represented as a whole person' (2011: 150), whilst Luzhin is fragmented, reduced to the feverish chess notations which are his entire focus. He is unaware that he has arrived at his destination, whilst Natalia is purposeful, organising the arrival of her mother who comments on her daughter's 'independence' in travelling alone across Europe.

It is Natalia whose gaze we share as it follows Luzhin's shambling and haphazard movements, and later his proficiency at chess, and Natalia who summarises for him his rambling account of his life: 'So: there was a short life before chess – about ten years. Then chess became your whole life. And then, there was the day before yesterday.' 'Yes', he affirms, 'When we met'. Echoing Clarissa, Natalia accepts Luzhin because with him 'I can breathe', and we get a clear sense of the alternative she faces in the attentions of Jean de Stassard (Christopher Thompson), a character not in Nabokov's novel. De Stassard is the suitor preferred by her mother whose courtship involves finding out 'everything about you' – his list comprises all the cultural experiences expected of a young woman of her class – and who persistently interrupts and seeks to reverse her contemplation of Luzhin. Natalia, however, is a far more active figure than Clarissa, responding with irony to de Stassard, and drawing Luzhin into a world of the body and its rhythms that echoes that of Antonia. Dance, as we have seen, functions in two ways in Gorris's films. As formal social ritual, it enacts the gendered power structures of a patriarchal society, but as embodied connection it can subvert them, suspending linear time in the shared performance of bodily movement. For Antonia, it represented life: 'Life's got to be lived', she says. 'This is the only dance we dance'. Here, unlike in Nabokov's novel, Luzhin is given a capacity for dance glimpsed in our, and Natalia's, early views of him crossing space, where his shambling gait breaks into sudden brief twirls.

It is after the return of Valentinov and his renewed infantilisation of Luzhin that Natalia coaxes him into dance. In a scene that recalls a sequence from *Broken Mirrors* in which Diane is faced with a client who lies, curled like an infant, weeping on the bed, she finds Luzhin similarly prostrate and in tears. In the earlier film Diane withdrew her gesture of comfort, finding it impossible within the structure in which she found herself. Here, however, Natalia comforts Luzhin as she would a child, addressing him as his father did, as Sasha. The invitation she goes on to extend to him, however, first to dance and then to sex, is to a full and joyful engagement with, and acknowledgement of, the body. 'You have to make brilliant, bold, courageous moves', she says, echoing his language of chess, but these are rhythmic moves of the body, shared and, in the montage of their movements that follows, increasingly fluid. The film playfully cuts between Luzhin's resulting successes in the tournament and the couple's increasing sexual pleasure, but just as Natalia initiated the sequence, it is on the image of *her* smilingly reflective face that it ends.

Natalia's invitation comes after she has opened the window of Luzhin's room. As she looks down we share her gaze at the giant chessboard set out on the lawn below, on which three couples are dancing. It is Natalia, not Luzhin, who in Gorris's film sees a chessboard spread out below, and what she sees is the stiff immobility of its ranked pieces contrasting with the fluidity of the couples' movements across it. Natalia's invitation is to a closeness centred on vulnerability and touch, and the pleasure of a shared corporeality. She does not demand that he abandon chess (it is the psychiatrist

Figure 3.4 The dance

who will insist on this), but she does want to break the hold of its rigid abstraction and release him into life – 'the only dance we dance'. Later, as he recovers from his breakdown in the sanatorium, it is not safety and domesticity that she proposes for their future, as in Nabokov's novel, but 'a new direction'. In response, he repeats her earlier summary of his life ('A short life before chess . . .') but now characterises the years of chess as 'the lost years'. It is a response which, together with the new awareness of his surroundings that he now displays, suggests that such a change might be possible.

In Nabokov's novel, Luzhin dies seeing below him, spread out 'obligingly and inexorably' (Nabokov [1964] 1994: 179), an eternity of chess squares, 'the same world he touched during the peak moments of his games' (Alexandrov 1991: 82). Both obsession and transcendence, it is chess that recaptures him as he falls. Luzhin's final leap from the window in Gorris's film is rather different. Here it is not chess squares that he sees – Natalia's vision of the chessboard below, with all its prosaic limitations, is the one we have been invited to share. Instead Luzhin sees the rollercoaster whose exhilaration he experienced before his aunt substituted for it her present of a chess set; gazing upwards, not down into the 'chasm', it is this remembered freedom towards which he leaps. Setting out for his wedding he has again been kidnapped by Valentinov, who has set up a continuation of the match with Turati. He throws himself from the car but is once more unable to navigate his surroundings, seeing only the return of an earlier chess pattern ('No it's a wrong move. An obvious move'). Locking himself in his hotel room, he fails to hear Natalia's calls to him, interpreting her knocking as that of his father, whose voice alternately forbids him chess and once again invites him, like 'Pushkin's doomed duellist', to begin their game. His final leap of escape is an attempt to grasp life, not transcendence.

Completing the game

The narrative of *Luzhin's Defence*, writes Belén Vidal, 'unfolds like an extended chess game which is finally given sense – and a sense of closure' (2005: 264) by the move in which Natalia completes the game with Turati. The analogy she suggests is one first proposed by Nabokov himself, who writes of endowing the elements of his narrative 'with the semblance of a game of skill . . . a regular chess attack' ([1964] 1994: viii). Gorris does indeed tease us with Nabokov's metaphor: her narrative contains repetitions, 'false moves', attacks and attempts at 'defence'. If we follow it, Natalia becomes the white queen, mobile and brave, taking on Luzhin's opponent, Valentinov, in his defence. After her initial meeting with Luzhin she appears always in light-coloured clothing, and when her parents burst in on her to dissuade her from marrying Luzhin and find her posed before a cheval mirror in her wedding dress, she seems to have become the queen to the king whose 'moves are limited' that he represents. Throughout the film, whilst Luzhin is found in dark, oppressive, closed-in rooms, Natalia moves confidently through space, never confined. When after their abandoned wedding she races to attempt to prevent his suicide and then sits, defeated, in his room with the glass chess king ('so much a part of you') beside her, still wearing her wedding dress, she seems the very embodiment of the queen that Luzhin's aunt described. Indeed, to the extent that Natalia is constrained by the structures around her – the social conventions that require the wedding and her separation from Luzhin before it, the wider structures that demand that she choose a husband, and beyond them the Europe of the interwar period with its hints of the fascist domination to come – the metaphor holds. For all her agility and bravery, the world in which she moves imposes constraints; being able to 'breathe' within them, as Clarissa found, is a precarious and limited achievement.

As Gorris suggests in her playful opening to the film, however, with its black and white series of tunnels set against the mobility and colour of Natalia's entrance, the masculine preoccupation with chess offers a limited and inadequate vision. Gorris, as Vidal also argues in her account of the film (2005: 270), appropriates Nabokov's narrative and, as with *Mrs Dalloway*, repositions it and its creator within the historical context that the novel itself, with its claims to timelessness, relegates to the margins. The emigré world of chess, trains and lakeside hotels was also that of Nabokov (Mazierska 2011: 158), and the chess patterns into which both author and protagonist retreat are simply a repetition in abstract form of the structures of violence and domination which are their context. Gorris, as the film's hostile reviewers were uneasily aware, usurps the position of author, telling the story from somewhere else; Natalia is her creation and her avatar. She completes the game with Turati, shakes hands and walks away, her gaze focused beyond the social and narrative structures that have constrained her – beyond, too, the frame of the 'heritage film' through which Gorris has reimagined his story.

This Natalia of the film's closing sequences is an anachronistic figure, taking on and defeating the all-male world of chess, triumphantly completing the world championship game with Turati but walking away from it, and compelling her defeated opponent, who seeks to congratulate her by kissing her hand, to shake hands instead. It is an ending that recalls those of *A Question of Silence* and *The Last Island*: a 'What if' that points beyond the narrative and the world depicted in the film to other possibilities. It is prepared for, once again, through the image of a boat, this time bearing Luzhin's coffin as it slowly crosses the misty lake, all surrounding context obliterated by the mist and the only sound that of its oars in the water. As a bell begins to toll in the distance the shot that follows, a surreal image of a silent and motionless group of mourners arranged, with the exception of Natalia, symmetrically in pairs in front of a castellated wall, might perhaps alert us to the narrative break that this sequence represents. It ends on a close-up of Natalia's face, held for almost twelve seconds, as she gazes towards the camera, perhaps at the approaching boat, perhaps at the rewritten ending – the 'What if' – that we are about to see.

Feminised worlds?

The heritage film, as Julianne Pidduck writes, is a 'quintessentially "feminine" genre' (2004: 16), often based on 'literary' sources, characterised by its period settings, its opulent and static mise-en-scène, its elaborate costumes and period detail, and its focus on upper-middle-class privilege (Vidal 2012: 8). For Gorris, however, the world of her two 'heritage films' is as patriarchal as that she depicts elsewhere; she is insistent that these adaptations are as much about 'the survival of women in a patriarchal world' as are her more obviously 'authored' films (Gorris 2023). The difference is that here their female protagonists must survive alone. Both films are adaptations of modernist literary texts, written and set in the 1920s but with claims – though differently asserted – to a certain timelessness. In placing them so firmly in a costumed past, Gorris positions both their narratives and the authors of her source texts within a world of affluent interwar settings and elaborate social rituals beneath which we can glimpse the brutality and restrictions of a patriarchal and class-based society. Its most obvious symbols are the World War I veterans who haunt the streets in Mrs Dalloway and the fascist soldiers in the background of The Luzhin Defence, but both films emphasise restriction and the domination of a rigid social and political order. In both, the moneyed élite that they depict has learnt nothing from past war and revolution and will lead Europe into the horror which we, but not the authors of the source texts, know is to come, a horror against which the counter-vision of *Antonia's Line* unfolded.

These costumed worlds are suffocating, and the films' female protagonists are without the support of a community of women through which the possibility of resistance was created in Gorris's earlier films. In *Mrs Dalloway* this possibility was glimpsed briefly in Clarissa's relationship with Sally, through the narrative pauses through which it was explored, with their suggestions of a shared corporeal openness and vulnerability. In *The Luzhin Defence* Natalia seeks it in her relationship with Luzhin, a vulnerable man exploited and feminised by patriarchal control, in whom the possibility of an openness to life can be seen in his sudden, solitary irruptions into dance. Though briefly joyful, the relationship is not enough. Luzhin is unable, as Vidal (2005: 265) writes, to escape both his history and 'the confines of a world defined by the implacable logic of chess', a world which mirrors in abstract form the structures around him. At the end of the film Natalia walks decisively out of both Luzhin's world and the framing of his (and her) story that Nabokov imposed. Stripped of context – the camera is entirely focused on Natalia's body and face – the final shot seems also to leave behind the genre of the heritage film. As with Joanna in *The Last Island*, the film has raised the possibility that she is pregnant: her mother accusingly suggests it and, more importantly, we see Natalia cup her belly protectively after the shock of Luzhin's suicide. Like Joanna, she carries into the future hope and life – there is, as Mrs Godame reminded us, 'nothing else' – and it is on this optimistic note that the film ends. Gorris's 'What if' final act to the narrative has meant that *The Luzhin Defence*, despite its origins in Nabokov's misogynistic vision, suggests the possibility of an elsewhere and another story, rather than, as *Mrs Dalloway* does, finding this possibility in an already closed-off past. It is, however, a solitary triumph. Julianne Pidduck has pointed to a similar rewriting of the endings of adapted novels in the films of Jane Campion (*The Portrait of a Lady* 1996), Patricia Rozema (*Mansfield Park* 1999) and Agnieszka Holland

(*Washington Square* 1997), seeing them as feminist 'gesture[s] towards the future' which are, however, limited by their focus on 'female (and protofeminist) *individuals*' (Pidduck 2004: 110, my italics). *The Luzhin Defence* repeats this gesture but makes us aware of Natalia's isolation: despite her confident gaze outward, towards the present, Natalia is without the female support that nurtured the protagonists of Gorris's earlier films.

Notes

1 Citron further characterises this power as 'the opportunity to reach a larger audience, the potential of using mainstream culture to critique or subvert it, the freedom to define and test one's own personal boundaries as film-maker'. The price is loss of control to the producer and distributor (1988: 57).

2 Geraghty is quoting from Peter Ackroyd in the *Spectator*, reviewing *Swann in Love* (1984).

3 Wilmington (1998).

4 Though the words come from Woolf, the scene also recalls the ending of another 'woman's film', *Brief Encounter* (1945) in which Laura (Celia Johnson) is also preserved from danger (the danger of an affair) and 'gradually revives' in the calm presence of her *Times*-reading husband, Fred (Cyril Raymond).

5 In *A Room of One's Own* she writes:

> If one is a woman one is often surprised by a sudden splitting off of consciousness, say in walking down Whitehall, when from being the natural inheritor of that civilization, she becomes, on the contrary, outside of it, alien and critical. ([1929] 1993: 88)

6 The film's DoP was Bernard Lutic. Gorris notes that 'He shot the film himself (most DoP's don't) like a ballet dancer, I thought. He was so agile and versatile. He was French, and though my French is no more than adequate, we were hand in glove' (Gorris 2024).

7 Subtitled 'An Essay on the Limits of Painting and Poetry ', Lessing's *Laocoön* is seen as the first extended attempt in modern times to define the distinctive spheres of art and poetry.

8 Joanne Pidduck points out (2004: 94) that in costume biopics of great (male) artists a close-up of the hand is often used to convey 'the difficult business of self-expression'. Here it indicates the claustrophobic narrowness of Luzhin's world.

4

Abject zones and liminal worlds

> The important theme in all my films is the survival of women in a patriarchal world. That is not only the case in the scripts I wrote myself but also in *Mrs Dalloway, The Luzhin Defence, Carolina*, and finally *Into the Whirlwind*. (Gorris 2023)

Gorris's final two films, *Carolina* (2003) and *Into the Whirlwind* (2008), return, though in very different ways, to the vision that grounded resistance and agency in her early films: that of a female-centred community whose subjects are marginalised and vulnerable but agentic and defined by an ethics of care. Unlike her early films, however, neither was from a script originated by Gorris. She was finding it increasingly difficult to get films made, and both productions were, she reports, 'fraught with difficulties' (ibid.). The two films were produced in very different circumstances – *Carolina* with Hollywood financing[1] and *Within the Whirlwind* through precarious international co-funding – but neither received cinema distribution.

Carolina (2003)

> I don't think I ever quite got the hang of Hollywood. (Gorris 2023)

Described on the English-language DVD cover as 'an endearing romantic comedy', *Carolina* follows Carolina Mirabeau (Julia Stiles) as she tries to reconcile her ambitions to have a successful career in television and meet 'a normal, available guy' with the centrality in her life of what the DVD cover calls 'her wacky Southern family', headed by her grandmother Millicent (Shirley MacLaine). During the dating show on which she works in Los Angeles she meets an upper-middle-class Englishman, Heath Pierson (Edward Atterton), who appears to embody this ideal, and he invites her out. Introduced at their annual Christmas celebration to her family, which includes her younger sisters Georgia (Azura Skye), who is pregnant, and Maine (Mika Boorem), her alcoholic father Teddy (Randy Quaid) and Aunt Marilyn (Jennifer Coolidge) who runs a brothel, Heath leaves early and breaks off contact with Carolina. In contrast, her city neighbour and 'best friend' Albert Morris (Alessandro Nivola), a romance novelist who writes under the pseudonym of Daphne St. Claire, accepts and is accepted by her family. Albert declares his love for Carolina, revealing that he has written a romantic novel dedicated to her under his own name, but she responds with surprise and confusion. Grandma Mirabeau is killed in a car accident and Carolina realises that Albert is the man she has been searching for, but he rejects her. Three months later, Carolina has taken her grandmother's place at the head of the extended outdoor family table, as they celebrate Thanksgiving. Albert appears and they kiss, to the delight of Grandma Mirabeau, whose ghost appears to Carolina.

An endearing romantic comedy

As this synopsis makes clear, the film contains the familiar narrative elements of the romantic comedy, summarised by Claire Mortimer as 'boy meets girl, various obstacles prevent them from being together, coincidences and complications ensue, ultimately leading to the couple's realisation that they were meant to be together' (2010: 4). Common situations, she adds, include 'mistaken identity, disguise and masquerade, intimate tête-à-têtes (often meals), public humiliation' and 'confiding in friends' (ibid.: 5) – all of which the film includes. In particular, *Carolina* conforms to the third of Mortimer's narrative models for the genre,[2] in which 'One half of the couple realises their love for the other early on, but the other half is slow to recognise and return their love, often having to lose the wrong partner in order to be ready for the right love' (ibid.: 5).

The DVD cover positions the film even more precisely. Its combination of familiar romance plot, career-minded young woman and eccentric Southern family produces, it declares, a film that is '[a]s funny and charming as *Sweet Home Alabama*', a number-one box-office success from the previous year. There, too, an ambitious young woman (Reece Witherspoon) meets her ideal man in the city – here New York – but ultimately finds both romantic happiness and her true identity in acknowledging her Southern roots.

Carolina, then, was produced as part of the upsurge in romantic comedies that Frank Krutnik identifies as appearing from the mid-1980s and growing in number throughout the 1990s: films, he writes, that sought 'to reconcile old-fashioned romance' with the sexual liberalisation of those years (2002: 138). Self-reflexive and citational, invoking 'keynote romantic texts of the past' and often featuring a 'deception narrative' (ibid.: 142), these 'new romances' for Krutnik simultaneously play with and reinforce the traditional conventions of the romantic comedy, producing narratives that ultimately function to 'contain and domesticate' any threatened rebellion from their female protagonists (ibid.: 143). Always identified as a 'woman's genre', the romcoms of the 1990s and 2000s now focus increasingly on the perspectives and experiences of these protagonists (Deleyto 2009: 153), often centring friendships between young women and with a number scripted and/or directed by women.[3] As Diane Negra writes in her highly critical account, however, this embrace of female relation-ships in the 'chick flick' is accompanied by an implicit or explicit rejection of feminism. For Negra (2009: 8, 17), the romantic comedies of the 1990s and 2000s speak 'from and to a neoconser-vative cultural context' in which the 'postfeminist promise' they offer of finding oneself through the operation of 'choice', a process they represent as empowering, is also a process of '"unlearn[ing]" feminism' through the rediscovery of the traditional values of family and hometown. 'Retreatist fantasies' (ibid.: 23), films like *Sweet Home Alabama* and *The Prince and Me* (2004), the film with which Julia Stiles followed *Carolina*, pit the glamour and wealth of a sophisticated cosmopolitanism, embodied in the film's 'Prince Charming' figure, against the solid warmth of the female protagonist's hometown family and community, epitomised in her mother. It is, argues Negra, a romanticisation of the hometown which centres on women's redomestication (ibid.: 16). Whilst it is the mother who, having herself been denied a career, has encouraged her daughter's ambition, it is she who now points out what her daughter has lost in pursuing it.

As the DVD cover suggests, *Carolina* includes many of the tropes familiar from these films. Indeed, its credited scriptwriter is Katherine Fugate, who went on to script *The Prince and Me*. The superficiality of Carolina's city life working on a TV dating show is contrasted with the rough warmth of her family, embodied in her grandmother. Carolina's cosmopolitan 'Prince Charming' – the term she uses when he pulls strings to get her reinstated after her family has caused her to be fired – is played by an English actor with a distinct resemblance to Colin Firth. *Bridget Jones's Diary* had been released in 2001, and Marleen Gorris notes that *Carolina* was originally intended to feature a 'not so very young girl' who, like Bridget, 'was afraid to be left on the shelf' (Gorris 2023). Like Bridget, Carolina is simultaneously cynical about romance ('Why are the women all princesses?' She asks Albert of his formulaic romance novels) and in search of her ideal man, with a history of 'always pick[ing] the wrong guy'. Albert is the longstanding friend whose love she fails to register, a feminised man who provides the film's elements of deception and gender inversion in his masquerade as romantic novelist Daphne St. Claire, and who finds self-knowledge in learning to embrace romance in his own name. Allusions to 'keynote romantic texts of the past' are provided by references to D. H. Lawrence and Tolstoy's *Anna Karenina*. After complications and confusions the film ends, as expected, with the union of the romantic couple, as they acknowledge their love with a kiss.

Carolina was not Gorris's first choice of project. Asked to take over from a director who had already started pre-production, she accepted because 'most of my other American projects had fallen through'. The film that was released to DVD was not her edit; the American producer, she reports, first fired her editor so that she was 'forced to work with someone from his own stable' and then, when she had returned to Amsterdam after finishing her director's cut, made further changes and deletions without her knowledge (Gorris 2023). This is, then, the film that is furthest from the fully authored nature of her early work where, as she writes, 'I . . . never had to make concessions, and when needed, I could change, rewrite and adapt as I went along. And I had the final cut' (ibid.). She did, however, make significant changes to the film she was handed, changes which point back to those early films and the vision they embody. Before examining them in detail, however, I want to return to the topic of romantic comedy and the possibilities it might offer to a feminist filmmaker like Gorris.

Comedy, carnival and the 'green world'

Mortimer's summary of the narrative structure of romantic comedy, quoted above, is a modified and softened version of that produced by Northrop Frye in 1957:

> What normally happens is that a young man wants a young woman, that his desire is resisted by some opposition, usually paternal, and that near the end of the play some twist in the plot enables the hero to have his will (Frye 1957: 163).

As Kathleen Rowe points out in her discussion of Frye's work, it is a formulation that is blind to the patriarchal nature of the structure it outlines, with its emphasis on Oedipal rebellion, but Rowe also emphasises elements of Frye's account that are useful to feminism. For Frye all comedy (and romance) is an attack on the established order – the Law of the Father – seeking to 'level, disrupt, and destroy hierarchy' (Rowe 1995: 101). In it, the characters 'who stand for the values of freedom, anarchy, and new life' defeat 'whatever stands for tradition, authority, rigidity, and death' (ibid.: 103). They do this through a temporary retreat into a magical space 'that Bakhtin would call the carnivalesque, Victor Turner the liminal' and Frye himself a 'green world' of nature, festivity and renewal (ibid.: 108). This 'other' world is a feminised space in which life triumphs over order and women may be 'unruly': subjects as well as objects of desire. At the close of the narrative the old world is renewed or transformed by contact with this other space, and this renewal is celebrated by a dance or feast.

In Rowe's introduction to the concept of the 'unruly woman' she cites *A Question of Silence* as an instance of a feminist use of 'female unruliness and the grotesque in a narrative about "very ordinary, very normal" women' (ibid.: 14), a narrative that finally explodes into a 'terrible and wonderful' (ibid.: 2) Medusan laughter.[4] Rowe's concept draws on Mary Russo's re-reading of Mikhail Bakhtin's theory of carnival. For Bakhtin, mediaeval carnival 'celebrated temporary liberation from the prevailing truth and from the established order'. It was 'the feast of becoming, change, and renewal', representing for the oppressed a 'utopian realm of community, freedom, equality, and abundance' ([1965] 1994a: 199). Its spaces were the streets and marketplace, not the institutional, hierarchical spaces of church, palace or private home, its people were the disorganised crowds, and its bodies were grotesque – 'open, protruding, extended, secreting' (Russo 1988: 219). These bodies were also, as Russo points out, typically female; and she sees in this fact – one not emphasised by Bakhtin – and in these bodies' accompanying characteristics of 'performance, imposture, and masquerade', the possibility of a new cultural politics for women (Bakhtin [1965] 1994b: 213). The unruly woman of Rowe's 'genres of laughter', then, is a figure of excess, creating 'disorder by dominating, or trying to dominate, men'. Her body and speech are out of control, she makes jokes at men's expense, she is often old but refuses to accept the invisibility of age, her sexuality is unfettered, and she is associated with liminality: 'threshold, borders, or margins' (Rowe 1995: 31). She is an ambivalent figure, at once a woman who 'creates a disruptive spectacle of herself' (ibid.) and inhabits what Anne McClintock (1995: 72) calls 'threshold' or 'abject' zones – zones, writes McClintock, such as the ghetto or slum, the brothel or the squatter camp – and at the same time a 'prototype of woman as subject' (Rowe 1995: 31).

In Rowe's later work she identifies *Antonia's Line* with a liberatory celebration of this figure and her world; it is, she writes, a film which presents 'a fully realized feminist utopia centered on a line of unruly girls and unrepentant mothers' (Rowe Karlyn 2011: 228). In it, the liminal or abject space of women's resistance has expanded to become the joyous, fertile world of the film, and the celebratory feast which for Frye signalled narrative resolution is recurrent, multi-generational and inclusive. *Antonia's Line*, as we have seen, references but refuses and critiques generic structures and tropes, 'pushing beyond', in Rowe Karlyn's words, the 'familiar genres of a woman's life' (ibid.: 233). *Carolina*, in contrast, despite the opening credits which claim it as 'A Marleen Gorris film', is firmly bound by the conventions of romantic comedy which enabled its financing, determined its marketing and casting – Julia Stiles was already under contract when Gorris began work on the film – and produced its final shape. It is a film that struggles to evade the constraints of this 'familiar genre of a woman's life', but Gorris is insistent that it shares the themes of her earlier work. *Carolina*, she says, 'was supposed to be a romantic comedy', but 'I shifted the emphasis . . . to the setting of a community of women against a lower-class background', with Shirley MacLaine 'as the genuine, bossy grandmother' at its centre (Gorris 2023). The result is a fractured and occasionally narratively incoherent film,[5] but one which, in what should be the margins of its central romantic narrative, offers both a critique of the postfeminist romantic comedy that it is 'supposed to be' and the suggestion of another possible world not unlike that of Antonia.

Threshold zones

Carolina opens with an upbeat pop-rock song, 'Get Over It', whose lyrics place us firmly in the sphere of dating and break-ups.

What we see, however, is not the fast-moving urban world of the post-1990 romance protagonist but a landscape of scrubland, pumpjacks and a half-derelict oil refinery, from which Grandma's beat-up car emerges to head down the hill and into the outskirts of Los Angeles. It is a marginalised landscape, on the edge of but outside and hidden from the city, dominated by the still-operational relics of the oil industry on which Los Angeles was founded but which the clean white lines of its urban centre disguise and disavow.[6] As the camera zooms in, we see Grandma Mirabeau's house on the hillside opposite, approached via a dirt track and surrounded by a now overgrown post-industrial wasteland. 'Boy, does your grandma live in a strange part of Los Angeles,' comments Albert later, as Carolina drives him to the latest of the Mirabeau family gatherings. Shots of the pumpjacks introduce these scenes and indicate the passing of time, their giant, deliberate movements overshadowing the Mirabeau family's reunions. On the sloping, roughly cleared area in front of the house, littered with broken furniture and burnt-out cars, its assorted members gather at tables assembled from doors balanced on car tyres and barely upright picnic tables, to celebrate Thanksgiving, Christmas and life.

Figure 4.1 Mirabeau family feast

This is not the 'green world' of Frye's account of romantic comedy, or the rural hometown America of its postfeminist successor. Rather, it is an abject zone as McClintock defines it: an unacknowledged borderland, one of industrial modernity's 'impossible edges' (McClintock 1995: 72), essential to its functioning but unseen and operating at the borders of legality. In the film's opening sequence, which introduces Grandma Mirabeau and the young Carolina and Georgia and sees baby Maine deposited by her father Theodor/Ted with his mother – the third daughter, of different mothers, to be left by him in her care – we see the family's dependence on the sale of illegal cigarettes for a precarious income. Ted's profession, we will learn, is that of 'drunk', Georgia has never had a job ('I didn't have the right shoes'), and Aunt Marilyn runs a brothel and is in and out of prison for credit-card fraud. Although the first scene's flashback to Carolina's childhood echoes that which begins *Sweet Home Alabama*, this is a very different world from that of the romanticised South of that film, with its conservative (white) family values and nostalgia for a lost Confederate identity. In the opposition drawn there and elsewhere between what Negra calls 'the venal, sexually unstable culture' of the city and 'an idealized American hometown' (2009: 19), the world of Gorris's film is invisible, impossible. The people who gather here are disparate, an accumulated not a biological family, which includes Aunt Marilyn's 'hookers', Grandma's married lover and the Chinese worker who is the father of Georgia's baby. Like Antonia's, this is a community of society's marginalised and rejected, with an openness and warmth that recalls that of Gorris's earlier film. Its members' stories are not developed as they are in *Antonia's Line*, so that the temporal rhythms of its scenes are constantly truncated by the demands of the romance plot, but extended shots of their weathered faces suggest something of their lives, and in one case, where we see a middle-aged woman in European farm costume looking back at the camera, we are offered an explicit reminder of Antonia herself.

Like Antonia's, this is a matriarchal world, and Grandma Mirabeau is the 'unruly woman' of Rowe's description: excessive, disruptive, spectacular, blunt and scatalogical in her speech, and with an unrepressed sexuality. In her refusal to allow the abortion of the unborn Carolina she was, says her younger sister Marilyn, 'like a fiery, winged banshee from hell'. To the adult Carolina Grandma says, in an echo of Antonia and Mrs Godame, 'Now, after a while you learn that the rules of the world don't have to apply to you. It's all nonsense. We're here; we die'. In its scenes of festive celebration we see the inclusiveness of this world, and in those between the three sisters Carolina, Georgia and Maine we see the fullest expression of its warmth. As they celebrate New Year's Eve together the soundtrack music tells us that 'The night can seem to last forever', but this is not a night of romance, or of preparation for it or regret at its absence. Instead, the accompanying montage gives us the sisters' physical closeness, support and comfort, tears, dance and play, with the camera taking us in close enough to catch the hint of tears and feel the embrace of bodies. Dance, writes Frye, is the traditional symbol for time not as 'fatality and destruction' but as 'energy, exuberance, and [a] kind of genuine freedom' (1976: 153). Gorris used dance in this way in *Antonia's Line*. In *Carolina* this sense of time is only glimpsed, but in this and later scenes where the three sisters sit entwined together after Grandma Mirabeau's death, it is clear that these relationships, rather than the romance narrative, are the film's centre.

Figure 4.2 The sisters

Romance and the city

The romcom, writes Mortimer, features 'urban settings, domestic spaces, often desirable apartments, restaurants and other social spaces' (2010: 9). This is the world to which the film introduces us after the flashback to Carolina's childhood. It is not, however, the world of the successful fashion designer of *Sweet Home Alabama* or the star science student of *The Prince and Me*, careers against which the postfeminist retreatist fantasies of Negra's account pit the allure of hometown and/or romance. Carolina is floor manager on a cheap and derivative dating show whose host, at first apparently merely comically egotistic, is revealed to be also ruthlessly powerful when he fires her – hers simply one in a series of similar firings. A montage of the recorded self-presentations of its would-be contestants, all men looking for women, reveals a similar level of monstrous and potentially violent self-absorption; from their dates they demand only anonymity ('I don't want to ever know her name'), a 'good job', and 'good breasts'. Against this background of misogyny Heath Pierson, self-deprecating and believing that 'men and women should be equal partners', stands out, but it is quickly clear that his ease with a theoretical female equality is born of privilege: dinner, he thinks, can assuage for Carolina the loss of her job ('You must be from a rich family', she says. 'I thought so'). When he makes 'a few calls' to get her reinstated, the gendered and class power behind what Carolina calls 'this Prince Charming kind of stuff – to the rescue and all that' is fully evident.

This is the 'patriarchal world' in which Gorris's protagonist seeks to survive: a world in which heterosexual romance is the promise through which consumer goods are sold (Heath's power comes from his role as an advertising executive) and women are both audience and objects of exchange. It is a world against whose falseness the romantic comedy structure sets Albert, the supportive 'best friend' who has not had sex with Carolina because, he says, in an echo of *When Harry Met Sally* (1989), 'friends and sex don't mix',[7] but who is in fact in love with her.

Albert, however, is also a cynical purveyor of what Lauren Berlant (2008: 35) calls the 'gendering machine' of women's genres. His female readers stand in line to have their copies of his books signed by an actress whom he pays to be his stand-in. His novels' heroes are pirates and rogue aristocrats who abduct their passive but willing victims – princesses all. When Carolina supplies Albert with possible next lines for his current book – 'She caresses his throbbing manhood'; 'She removes her bodice with trembling hands'; 'His hands slowly roam his newly conquered territory' – their shared play with the romance genre masks a structural inequality in which the stakes for Carolina in colluding with these formulations are very different from those for Albert. Berlant writes that 'popular culture constantly reinvents the love plot as a figure for optimism, while maintaining women's culture's strong ambivalence about believing in and relinquishing [its] promise' (ibid.: 171). Carolina shares this ambivalence and optimism, but Gorris's film makes it clear that the genres that induce it are produced by, and in the interests of, a capitalist patriarchal culture.

Albert's redemption, and that of the promise of romantic love, is to be achieved through the novel that he writes in his own name, in which he acknowledges his love for Carolina. What the film offers us, however, is an empty opposition. The extract we hear from Albert's novel is couched as much in the clichés of popular romance, if in more 'everyday' fashion (the book's title is *Everyday Magic*), as the text of his Daphne St. Claire novels. As Carolina watches Albert read from the novel to another rapt female audience, the scene is interrupted by the telephone call that informs her of her grandmother's death, returning her from the fantasy of herself as romance heroine – Albert's fantasy, in which she is invited to immerse herself – to the grim reality of her powerlessness. A long shot sees her walk through the poorly lit car-repair shop where she must pick up her grandmother's belongings, our view partially blocked by an imprisoning steel mesh, the hulking shapes of cars and the men who repair, inspect and buy them. It is a sequence which seems to be from a different, altogether bleaker film. The man behind the counter grille refuses to hand her the brown envelope of belongings without a cash payment, despite her emotional appeals: 'Sorry for your loss, but I'm running a business here'. It is the woman who sits behind him, silently typing, who finally hands Carolina her grandmother's effects and meets her eyes, in an unspoken gesture of solidarity which echoes those in Gorris's early films.

Festivity and renewal

The rest of the film, apart from two brief scenes in which Carolina informs Albert of Grandma Mirabeau's death by telephone and he rejects her attempt to reconsider his earlier declaration, remains in Grandma's liminal world, returning us finally to the celebratory feast which has punctuated the film. For Frye, Rowe writes, this 'magical place' was a 'world of festivity and natural renewal set apart from the ... world of history and politics' (1995: 108). In *Carolina*, against the pumpjacks which dominate its landscape we see once more the closeness of the sisters, the renewal of life in Georgia's baby and the resolution of the narrative sub-plot featuring Maine. It is Maine, the youngest sister, who introduced the film's references to D. H. Lawrence. Though she is given one brief scene in which she asks Aunt Marilyn about *Lady Chatterley's Lover*, however, the references are to a very different work by Lawrence, the short story 'The Rocking Horse Winner'. In it, a boy is driven to death by his desire to provide the money his parents' lifestyle demands. Riding his rocking horse, he has visions of racing winners, but his family's demand for ever more money drives him to madness and death, though not before he has predicted the winner of the Derby and secured a fortune for his parents. Repeating his actions, Maine uses her own rocking horse to predict lottery numbers, and then the date on which she should buy her ticket. Her grandmother, it is revealed, was on her way to buy the winning ticket when she was killed.

In Lawrence's tale, the boy dies trying to service his parents' conspicuous consumption. In Gorris's appropriation of Lawrence's dark fable the winning ticket is not bought, and what is important to Maine is that her grandmother believed in her and 'that I was right, and I'm not going crazy'. Like Danielle's visions in *Antonia's Line*, those of Maine comprise part of the inclusive and slightly magical nature of this matriarchal world, dreams that she must learn to harness. It is a world over which Grandma Mirabeau continues to preside after her death, through the non-realist flashback scenes which illustrate Aunt Marilyn's story of Carolina's birth. Like Antonia, Grandma loads a rifle to defend her family against the patriarchal society beyond, but now in comic mode. Her final appearance, conjured, it would seem, by Carolina as, like Antonia and granddaughter Sarah, they share a gaze across the communal table of the film's conclusion, is the image that closes the film.

In the postfeminist romantic comedies that Diane Negra describes, the female protagonist reaches what is presented as a compromise: she will maintain what Negra calls (2009: 95) an 'adjusted' career whilst embracing the traditional values of home and family. Compromise is an essential part, too, of Frye's vision of the romantic comedy's ending. The feast that marks the lovers' return to society and the 'real' world is, he writes, 'anti-utopian' (1976: 149), signalling the renewal, not the overturning, of the social world. *Carolina*, too, ends on compromise. Arriving at the feast over which Carolina is now presiding in her grandmother's place, Albert interrupts and then completes her speech with his own assertion that he intends to continue coming to the family gatherings 'for the next fifty years'. He kisses Carolina, there is a pause, and then she kisses him, looking over his shoulder at the vision of Grandma Mirabeau which she and we see. This is not, then, a compromise between career and romance, the urban and the 'hometown', though we learn that Carolina will continue her career, now as a documentary researcher. It is a compromise between the romance narrative and the matriarchal world that has decentred it throughout the film. Albert will be admitted to the feast, but it takes place in Carolina's world; she is now its centre, and the most powerful relationship remains that between her and Grandma Mirabeau, and all that she represents.

Kathleen Rowe Karlyn celebrates *Antonia's Line* as the expression of a 'wicked powerful feminism' that 'imagines the possibility of unruly girls and unrepentant mothers in relationships defined by mutual support' and by 'an ethos of care which flows not simply towards the next generation, but more universally towards the weak and vulnerable' (2011: 250). This is the vision that *Carolina*, too, seeks to offer. But the unruly woman of comedy is not the creator of a radically different social order. Traditionally a grotesque figure, she is a creator of disorder and excess, and the flamboyant excesses of Grandma Mirabeau place her within this tradition. The rhythms of her world, with its celebration of life, never quite establish themselves as dominant. Romantic comedy requires the restoration of gendered order and the celebration of the admission of the heterosexual couple into the established social world. The excessive older woman must be tamed or excluded. It is a conclusion that Gorris's film seeks to refuse. Grandma Mirabeau's marginalised and inclusive world will continue, slightly modified by Carolina's desire for order. But it remains marginal, the excluded other of the 'real' world of contemporary urban society. Carolina, the most conformist of the three granddaughters, is an unconvincing heir to her grandmother. Her silent acceptance of Albert's proprietorial kiss returns her to the conventions of romantic comedy,[8] despite her final exchange of looks with her unruly grandmother. Gorris's own compromise between these conventions and her vision of a female-centred community characterised by both vulnerability and resistance is similarly uneasy. The final words of *Antonia's Line* remind us that 'nothing has come to an end'; Antonia's great-granddaughter Sarah has been our narrator, and she will continue to write her world, a world into which we are invited. Those of *Carolina* belong to Albert; the ghost of Grandma Mirabeau fades as we watch.

Within the Whirlwind (2009)

Within the Whirlwind is based on a two-volume memoir by Eugenia Ginzburg, a university professor and Communist Party member from Kazan, who was arrested, tried and sentenced during Stalin's purges of the 1930s, and then spent eighteen years in prisons and Siberian labour camps. Born in 1904, Ginzburg taught history and Marxism-Leninism in Kazan colleges as well as working as a journalist for the newspaper *Red Tartary*. At the time of her arrest she was married to a senior member of the Kazan Regional Party Committee and had two small sons, one of whom later died of starvation during the siege of Leningrad. Rehabilitated in 1955, she unsuccessfully sought publication in Russia of the first volume of her memoir of Stalin's camps, *Journey into the Whirlwind*, seeing it published instead in Italy in 1967. The second volume, *Within the Whirlwind*, was published after her death in 1977, again in Italy. English translations were published in 1967 and 1981.

Traditional autobiographical writing, writes Annette Kuhn (2000: 180), is a genre in which 'a certain self, a particular identity, is constructed and made public'. As an account of the development of the writer/protagonist over time, it works to produce the narrator as a unified subject whose identity unfolds in historical time. Ginzburg's memoirs have been seen in this way: as a kind of *Bildungsroman* in which 'the neophyte attains political understanding, as well as a broader social experience' through her relations with women who share with her 'a prison cell or camp barracks' (Kelly 1994: 368). Indeed, this is how she herself sees them; she writes of her 'political naïveté' (Ginzburg 1967: 8) before her arrest, and later of her growing understanding during her period of imprisonment and exile not only of the extent of the horror of Stalin's purges but also of her own guilt. 'After all,' she writes, 'the assassin is not only he who struck the blow, but whoever supported evil, no matter how: by thoughtless repetition of dangerous political theories, by silently raising [her] right hand; by faint-heartedly writing half-truths. *Mea culpa*'

(1981: 153). What she depicts in the memoir, writes Dariusz Tolczyk, is a process of stripping back followed by reconstruction: 'a purposeful abandonment of her old moral framework of identity and the construction, almost from scratch, of a new one' (2005: 61). It is a process, he adds, in which she 'chooses vulnerability' as a means by which to 'undertake a lonely search for a new and more suitable moral language' (ibid.: 64). In this story of 'a mind purified by suffering' (Cooke 2023a), Ginzburg's is a journey whose means, development and outcome are clearly signalled in the text. When she meets the German doctor Anton Walter in the camp, we learn immediately of Walter's history, his character as 'a jolly saint' and that this 'jolly saint was to become my second husband' (1981: 108, 115). Similarly, the memoir's many characters serve as exemplars on her journey, and when they are introduced, we learn their ultimate fates as well as their histories and personalities. Ginzburg herself is able to achieve an aesthetic and moral distancing from her experiences through her ability to reference and quote from Russian literary classics, and it is this tradition in which she places herself. In her self-representation she becomes, writes Olga Cooke (2023b: xxvii), an embodiment of 'the features of the selfless heroine' of Russian literature.

Gorris's film follows the chronology of Ginzburg's memoir, beginning, as does *Journey into the Whirlwind*, with the time immediately before her arrest. Whilst the memoir itself continues until her rehabilitation and return to Moscow, however, the film ends after her release from the Elgen camp, with the aftermath recorded briefly at its close in screen text. It compresses Ginzburg's experiences across different prisons and camps, but retains key events and dialogue. With a script by American Nancy Larson and with German, Polish, French and Belgian producers, its production, unlike that of *Carolina*, was fraught with financial difficulties. It did, though, give Gorris back much of the control she had had in her earlier films. Listed as 'script editor' in the film's closing credits, she reports (2023) that she 'took some liberties' with Larson's original script. Like *Carolina*, however, the film was not given cinematic distribution, the result, according to its star Emily Watson, of being 'delivered pretty much the day the market crashed' (Rees 2011). Gorris herself reports that, as with most of her films, 'I had no idea what happened to the finished film . . . (as usual) I had no influence on its distribution' (Gorris 2023).

Within the Whirlwind, then, follows the chronology and detail of Ginzburg's memoir – its acknowledgement of the help of Ginzburg's adopted daughter, Antonina, in the closing credits speaks to this fidelity. Its vision, however, is distinctly different, and returns us to the themes of Gorris's early films. Here once more is a vision of resistance grounded in an embodied and shared vulnerability, and lived as endurance and care within an abjected, feminised space. Here, too, there is a return to questions of temporality and to the ways in which narrative film might represent alternative, female-centred modes of living with and within time. The film begins, however, firmly within historical time.

'It was all a long time ago, and it never happened anyway'

In Julia Kristeva's 'Women's Time', she argues that the first phase of the women's movement is characterised by women's aspiration to 'gain a place in linear time as the time of project and history'. It is a desire – for equal pay, professional recognition, contraception, abortion – which is bound up, she writes, with the rationality and values of the nation state, and it is one that she sees as having been largely fulfilled within the 'socialist countries of Eastern Europe' ([1979] 1986a: 193, 196). It is this world that we see at the beginning of *Within the Whirlwind*. We are informed at the film's opening that the date is 1934, and the place Kazan in the Soviet Union. The childlike song that opens the film tells us that Stalin is in power. We quickly learn of the assassination of Sergei Kirov,[9] and in a series of short scenes we witness the consequences of Stalin's purge of Party members that follows.

The Eugenia Ginzburg (Emily Watson) that we see in these opening scenes is a woman who, as Kristeva describes, has sought and won 'a place in linear time as the time of project and history' ([1979] 1986a: 193). She is a professor at Kazan University and writer for the *Red Tartary* newspaper, a Party member and wife of a senior local Party official. She is also a figure of modernity: smart, fashionable, at ease and in command in the workplace; sharing parental duties at home. When Stalin's purges begin, and she faces accusations of lack of political vigilance for not denouncing her colleague Yelvov (Pearce Quigley), her response is based on an appeal to a rational state order: '*Nobody* has spoken out against Yelvov . . . the district authorities put their trust in him and he was elected to the City Committee'. It also evinces a clear sense of self and status ('They can't possibly think that . . . They know that I work for the Party'), and of a moral rectitude which she identifies with the Party itself: 'I'm not guilty of anything. You want me to stand up there and tell *lies*? . . . I don't want to lie to the Party'. Modernity, writes Rita Felski, 'celebrates mobility, movement . . .', so that '[f]reedom and agency are . . . symbolized by movement through public space' (2000: 86). The Genia Ginzburg of the early part of the film is constantly in motion: striding confidently through streets and corridors and into lecture theatres, acknowledging in passing the admiration and deference of colleagues and students. When she paces across the lecture theatre, declaiming to her students a passage from Gogol's *Dead Souls* (1842), this movement becomes explicitly identified with a utopian vision of a progressive Russian nationalism: 'Up, up, up the horses dash', she declaims from memory; 'I love it, of course I do. I'm Russian. Give the horses their heads and to hell with the world!'[10] Genia, to quote Kristeva again ([1979] 1986a: 193), is fully identified with 'the socio-political life' and values of Soviet Russia.

With her arrest and imprisonment this sense of temporal order and progression is ruptured. Although historical events continue in the world beyond, Genia has no access to them or the actors in them. Time is first stopped – within her cell, where over a series of scenes nothing changes and she is forbidden even to pace, and in her repeated, almost identical interrogations by Party official Beylin (Ian Hart) – and then absurdly accelerated, when her trial takes just seven minutes from formal opening to sentencing. Once sentenced, however, her removal to the labour camp inaugurates a shift from this temporal rupture to an exploration of a different mode of temporality.

In this, the major portion of the film, the passing of time is rendered, as it was in *Antonia's Line*, as seasonal and diurnal change in landscapes shot in deep focus under vast skies. Dissolves map the slow change from a landscape deep in snow to one in which there are tentative signs of green, before snow covers all once again. Against this landscape, a slow procession of huddled human forms registers the women's circular journeys into the forest where they must work in temperatures of minus fifty degrees, and then back to the camp with its watch towers, huts and barbed wire. As in the earlier film, too, this is a temporality marked by scenes of repetition – of the women felling trees, or waiting in line for food – although here such routines carry always the threat of violation or death. It is also marked by small, and sometimes larger, gestures of care. 'Maintenance', writes Baraitser, 'is the temporal dimension of care' (2017: 53); here, the sharing of food or clothing, the bodily gestures of comfort or support, sustain Genia and the other women within this suspended time. Larger gestures preserve life and enact resistance in a more direct way – Genia steps in front of a guard's rifle to protect Lena; Lena (Agata Buzek) and Greta (Lena Stolze) similarly protect and support Genia after she learns of the death of her son – although sometimes, as with the nameless young woman in the food line who is shot when she turns and walks away, care is not enough.

Suspended moments

All of these elements of the film function to produce a sense of time slowed, and lived as endurance, maintenance, waiting, persisting. They also broaden the focus from an individual life narrated in retrospect – the memoir – to a wider and shared lived experience. Geetha Ramanathan has commented on the way that painting is used in *Antonia's Line* both to arrest the linear flow of narrative time and to authorise a mode of seeing that is more than merely subjective. Here, poetry performs a similar function. In Ginzburg's memoir, her frequent literary references serve to create a sense of intellectual distance from her surroundings, a way of maintaining her sense of self: 'Poetry, at least, they could not take away from me!', she writes; 'it was and remained mine' (1967: 221). They function too, as Olga Cooke writes (2023b: xxii), as the expression of 'a bittersweet urge to be part of a great pantheon of literary artists', and they are always contextualised and explained by the narrative voice. In Gorris's film, however, although the repetition of poetry aids Genia's survival, the way in which it does this is rather different.

In Western literary theory narrative and lyric poetry have been seen as invoking contrasting modes of temporality. Whilst narrative is characterised by temporal succession, writes Monique Morgan, lyric poetry is marked by its absence, by a sense of atemporality: of 'absolute simultaneity in a suspended moment' (2009: 135). Lyric poetry, that is, arrests time, binding reader and poet in a merged 'I' which speaks of present experience. Whilst narrative is identified with the dominant mode of historical thinking, lyric poetry speaks to a complex, often ambivalent present in which 'both affirmation and exploitation [may be] audible at once' (Nealon 2007: 886). For Susan Stanford Friedman, the two modes are gendered. Women writers, she argues, have made use of 'lyric interruptions' to 'resist' the forward movement of plot and 'disrupt narrative patterns that reinscribe the social order' (1989: 169).

It is this function that the citations of lyric poems – a far narrower selection than the literary references found in the memoir – serve in Gorris's film. They begin with Genia's voiceover in the cell where she is held before trial, when she quotes from poems by Osip Mandelstam and Marina Tsvetaeva. These poems by writers who would themselves be victims of Stalin's purges[11] speak to an insistence on embodied experience and selfhood in circumstances of abject degradation ('Somebody gave me this body; What do I do with it now? . . . I'm alive and I breathe'; 'I breathed in the haydust of milky stars. . . . There are five good senses on earth'), as well as to Genia's immediate situation ('I'm still alive. That may be soon a sin . . . Perhaps this age is iron and all must fall'). But they also function as an interruption to narrative. The protagonist's voiceover is not, as it usually is in cinema, the extradiegetic narration of past experience from the vantage point of the present (the point of narrative closure), a process which, as Kuhn argues, establishes 'the narrator as a unitary ego' (2000: 180): the self who knows. Instead, it suspends time *within* the diegesis; as Jonathan Culler argues of lyric poetry, we are presented with 'a time of discourse rather than story' (2001: 165). Voiced by Genia, and run together, these fragments of poetry acquire a sense of multiple authorship across moments of time. When they are repeated later in the film, as several of the fragments are, these moments become linked in a pattern that pulls against our sense of narrative progression, emphasising instead the connections between these expanded and suspended moments.

Elsewhere, poems connect people as well as moments – Genia and Old Vlady (Heinz Lieven) share a poem, taking turns to voice its lines, as do Genia and Anton (Ulrich Tukur). The repetition by Genia of popular satirical sayings voiced initially by other women in the camp produces a similar sense of shared experience and shared voice, as well as emphasising the women's sense of suspended temporality. The first of these, 'It was all a long time ago, and it never happened anyway' is first spoken by Greta on the journey to the camp which introduces the community of women, herded together in the cramped space of the railway wagon which is taking them to Siberia. The second is voiced by Olga (Beata Fudalej) moments later and recounts a medical examination in which the patient is asked to 'breathe'; on being told that the patient has been sentenced under Stalin's Article 58[12] the doctor amends the instruction: 'Well in that case, don't breathe'. Both are repeated later in exchanges between Genia and Anton. Both appear in Ginzburg's memoir, but as examples of the 'pithy sayings' (1981: 20) of others. In Gorris's film they underscore a shared sense of time as frozen, and hence as both unbearable ('Don't breathe') and, in terms of history, unnarratable ('it never happened anyway').[13]

Acts of care

'Acts of maintenance are durational and repetitious', writes Lisa Baraitser, 'they may concern time that seems frozen or unbearable in its refusal to move on, and entail practices of bearing the state of nothing happening, or the inability to bring about tangible or obvious forms of change'. It is a time that concerns 'vulnerable states' in which we are reliant on the practices of others, and which emerge in relation to 'histories of oppression and resistance, and histories of power and agency' (2017: 51). It is a time, she suggests, that is lived '*in the feminine*' (ibid.: 79, original emphasis), but not in the monumental, essentialised form suggested by Kristeva in 'Women's Time'. In Gorris's film it is the unbearable, unnarratable other to historical time, a temporality lived within one of modernity's unacknowledged abject zones (McClintock 1995: 72).

As elsewhere in Gorris's films, historical time in *Within the Whirlwind* is identified with patriarchal institutions, from the Party and the military to the family, where Genia's husband (Benjamin Sadler), like Janine's in *A Question of Silence*, is chiefly concerned at how her behaviour will impact on his standing. As she seeks to overturn the initial charge of 'lack of political vigilance' against her, the early identification of this confident modern woman with the institutions within which she works falls away. The corridors through which she passes in Moscow are vast and isolating, and she is now a tiny figure. Her brief illusion of power when she thinks she has succeeded in her plea is quickly destroyed by her future interrogator Beylin, who swaggers past her with his military entourage in a demonstration of institutional power. Her trial, with its row of uniformed men who determine judgement in her absence, echoes that in *A Question of Silence*, though its surreal absurdity is here presented through the dreamlike magnifications and distortions of Genia's viewpoint, as she stands weak with hunger after her solitary confinement, and surrounded by guards. When she returns to Kazan it is as a hunched and weeping figure in a third-class carriage; her movement is now determined elsewhere.

After the opening sequences, public, historical time, with its structures of power and oppression, is glimpsed only at the margins of *Within the Whirlwind*, but its institutions are ever-present as determining structure and threat. They are also brutally, unpredictably present in their effects. Like *Antonia's Line*, the film insists on a continuity between these institutions of power and the individual acts of brutality which they sanction. The bartering of food for sex by the guards overseeing the women at work, to which Lena succumbs with ultimately lethal consequences, echoes the bargains struck in *Broken Mirrors* by another group of marginalised and invisible women. The sudden irruption of violence into the women's hut, as guards burst in in an act of mass rape, echoes both the constant threat and ultimate eruption of violence in *Broken Mirrors* and the rapes in *Antonia's Line*, where the rapist Pitte, too, is a soldier. The threats of death when the women speak back or – quite literally – step out of line are a version of the outcomes depicted in Gorris's earlier films.

To be deprived of historical time is to be deprived of identity. The women here are stripped of their markers of identity: Genia loses both her public identities as university teacher, Party member and wife of an important official, and her private identity as mother. They have lost professions, partners, parents and children. Genia is informed of the death of her son Alyosha in a letter from her mother which the camp official, torturing her, withholds for long moments. In this scene the suspension of time and narrative is figured as the registering of loss: in the long close-up of Genia's face as it registers a dawning fear and realisation, and in the shot which follows, where she stands for long moments immobile, unable to take the now-proffered letter.

If the abject space of the camp is a space of brutality, vulnerability and loss, however, it is also one in which time's suspension – modes of enduring, waiting, persisting – gives rise to practices of care which become a resistance grounded in the shared recognition of that vulnerability. The transition begins during the transportation of the women to the camp. In the cattle wagon Genia gradually becomes a part of this group, sharing water and experiences, the camera placing us among the women, approximating the touch of these many bodies. At a brief stop at an isolated country station, where the guards buy fruit and vegetables from the waiting countrywomen, Genia peers out through a gap between the truck's sliding doors. In one of the silent gestures of care that are found so often in Gorris's films, a young peasant woman approaches her with a small bowl of raspberries held to her chest. As they make eye-contact, she gives the bowl to Genia before gently touching her face. When Genia looks again she sees her son Alyosha, her image of loss, alongside the young woman, but this vision fades; it is the young woman who offers care and hope and the camera remains on her as the train pulls away.

Within the camp the communal hut becomes the kind of abject yet resistant space that we saw in *Broken Mirrors*: one not of women's own choosing, and at the service and under the control of men, but one in which a community of women support one another through bodily and emotional pain by jokes, touch and physical expressions of care. As in the earlier film, the camera places us among the women as they share time, gathering to wash clothes, to share stolen food and medicine or recovered clothing, or around a narrated story. Despite their differences and the bodily evidence of malnutrition and brutality that we see, the women share warmth and laughter. In these sequences Gorris's lighting and palette, with its dull browns

Figure 4.3 The women's hut

and greens and occasional patches of brightness where sunlight penetrates or candles illuminate, echo Dutch paintings of warm, communal peasant interiors. In Ginzburg's memoir her ability to recite Russian classics from memory is an individual feat to be admired by both prisoners and guards; in the film it becomes a form of sharing, generating laughter and raucous comments as Genia tells the story of Oblomov, a man too rich and indecisive to get out of bed.[14]

Care in this world takes the form of iterative acts of both sharing and resistance. Genia brings from the infirmary stolen food and 'liquid gold' – cod liver oil. In turn, she is given Lena's red dress to wear for her first meal with Anton, a dress that Lena herself acquired from a heap of recovered clothing and which has functioned for her as a symbol of her own sexual rebellion. After Lena's suicide, as Genia prepares to leave the camp on her release, she is wearing Lena's shawl. Genia's act of stepping in front of a guard's rifle to protect Lena when she collapses is later echoed by Lena in protection of Genia, and then again by Genia herself as she tries in vain to protect the young woman who turns to her calmly in the food line and smiles, then walks stiffly towards the barbed wire fence and is shot and killed.

Joy, and rage

As in *Antonia's Line,* the space and temporality depicted in *Within the Whirlwind,* unlike those of Gorris's first three films, can admit men, under certain conditions. In Ginzburg's memoir her relationship with Anton Walter is central to the second volume: 'What sets this narrative apart from all other camp memoirs', its 1981 book jacket tells us, 'is that it is essentially a love story'. Gorris's film retains the relationship, and it is Anton who speaks to the possibility of joy even amidst devastating loss. 'Still, there is joy' he says, when Genia asks him how he can bear the loss of his wife and daughters, who died in a transit camp, 'Like today'. But there is also joy when Genia stands in the middle of the spring landscape and gazes both beyond and, closing her eyes, within, or when she is permitted to play the piano and her face lights in a slow smile. The relationship with Anton, though important, is displaced from the central position it holds in the memoir. They meet in the infirmary of the camp where she lives with the group of women, not, as in the memoir, later, in a different camp where she sleeps in the infirmary itself, away from other prisoners. Their relationship begins not when she realises he is a 'saint', but when she learns that he too has suffered loss and is a prisoner without power: when their relationship is discovered he is summarily sent to the Shturmovoi mine. That this relationship is part of a larger network of care we see when Genia returns to the women's hut after their night together. She enters to Greta's whispered information that Lena has been given another five-year term, so that the baby she is expecting will be taken from her. As Genia takes Lena in her arms to comfort her, against the background of the other women's presence, the image both parallels and contrasts with the earlier image of the lovers' embrace. Later, Genia's parting from Anton when he is removed from the camp is echoed when she is released, in her own parting from the group of women whose gifts and embraces she receives. In both instances it is the touch of hands on which the camera focuses, and which has come to signify care.

If the film shifts Anton Walter's role in Genia's survival from that depicted in Ginzburg's memoir, it also changes the nature of that survival. The Genia of Ginzburg's self-representation has brief moments of furious rebellion in the early days of her imprisonment, but learns forgiveness. When asked to visit a prisoner who had earlier given false evidence against Walter and has now suffered a stroke, she at first refuses. When she does visit, it is to find him asking for forgiveness, which she grants; his repentance is evidence, she writes, that 'from the depths of moral savagery' there can come 'the cry *mea maxima culpa*' and that with this cry the patient can recover 'the right to call himself a human being' (1981: 145). In the film it is her former interrogator Beylin, now a prisoner and dying, who requests her visit. He fails to recognise her and has learned nothing: he is different from her, he says, because '*I am innocent*'. Her response is to bend over him and say with cold deliberation, 'May you rot in hell, you bastard. You're not going to get me, *ever*'. She leaves him to die. It is an anger familiar from Gorris's early films, from Diane's confrontation with the serial killer in *Broken Mirrors* to Antonia's cursing of the rapist Pitte, a reminder that the affective and physical relationships of care in this frozen and abjected time and space do not preclude a sustained anger against what Baraitser calls 'histories of oppression that return in the present again and again' (2017: 54).

Like *A Question of Silence* and *The Luzhin Defence*, *Within the Whirlwind* ends on a freeze-frame of the protagonist's face. Released, Genia finds herself once again alone. Anton is not there to meet her at the camp gates and we see her sit clutching her bundle of belongings in the vast snowy landscape, across a series of dissolves. We hear her voice reciting Mandelstam's poem 'Somebody gave me this body'[15] once more. This time, however, the lines referring to 'this prison of a world' are omitted, so that the poem with its lines, 'I'm alive and I breathe . . . When I move, when I breathe, I leave my mark', seems to echo Mrs Gadame's answer in *The Last Island* to the question, 'How do you stand it all?' 'I enjoy *life*', she says. 'There is, after all, nothing else'. As

Figure 4.4 *Within the Whirlwind*: ending

Genia walks forward once again through a blizzard of increasing force she sees Anton, and the two struggle towards each other. The film's final shot is of her face as she looks forward, out beyond the camera's frame. Although the text that follows returns her story to the past, the suspended present of the poem and final image suggests, as in *Antonia's Line*, that 'nothing has come to an end'.

Conclusion

One of the very few reviews of *Within the Whirlwind* that exist online, from the World Socialist Web Site, complains that after its opening scenes of Stalin's 'brutal machinery of suppression' the film is 'disappointing' (Reinhardt 2011). Instead of depicting the 'reality' of 'the catastrophe that befell Soviet society', writes the reviewer, a catastrophe of which Ginzburg's personal history is but part, the film's focus is instead on Gorris's habitual concern, the 'timeless' depiction of strong women. Despite its dismissal of the film, this is not entirely inaccurate, as the quotation which heads this chapter confirms. As in her earlier films, Gorris is concerned to explore the ways in which women might find spaces in the interstices of historical time – vulnerable, often abject spaces – in which other modes of living with each other and with time might be experienced. These, in Lisa Baraitser's words, are modes of 'waiting, staying, delaying, enduring, persisting, repeating, maintaining, preserving and remaining' (2017: 2): forms of time that do not flow or, in the imagined world of *Antonia's Line,* flow with a rhythm beyond that of historical time. Depicting them involves patterns of repetition and echoing, and finding ways of arresting or sidelining narrative flow, often through the citation of 'atemporal' art forms. The spaces within which they are lived in *Within the Whirlwind* are, as the film tells us, both unbearable and unnarratable within the terms of the historical account into which the reviewer seeks to fold them. The community of women that is depicted is not, however, 'timeless', as he suggests. The women's spaces depicted here echo those seen elsewhere in Gorris's films, but they are produced by, and in relation to, the specific power structures of the historical time represented. The Genia Ginzburg we see, more than Gorris's other protagonists, is vulnerable in both senses described by Judith Butler: initially to the ideological structures that enable her sense of identity, and then in the form of an embodied 'dependency on other bodies and networks of support' (Butler 2016: 16), a shared vulnerability that makes possible both community and resistance.

Notes

1 IMDb reports a budget of $15,000,000.

2 The other two are the couple being separated at the start of the film, only to be reunited by its close having realised that they still love each other, and the couple falling in love at first sight but being separated by factors beyond their control (Mortimer 2010: 5).

3 Among others, *The Prince and Me* was directed by Martha Coolidge, and *Bridget Jones's Diary* by Sharon Maguire. Nora Ephron wrote *When Harry Met Sally* (1989) and directed, as well as having writing credits on, *Sleepless in Seattle* (1993) and *You've Got Mail* (1998). Amy Heckerling wrote, directed and produced *Clueless* (1995); Nancy Meyers has directed romantic comedies from the 1980s onwards.

4 Rowe is referring to Hélène Cixous' 'The Laugh of the Medusa' (1980).

5 Reviewers of the DVD pointed to an unexplained gap of five months in the narrative, as well as other breaks in narrative flow.

6 The growth of Los Angeles was triggered by the discovery and exploitation of oil in the 1890s. The highly toxic pumpjacks and refineries used for extraction have been camouflaged or phased out in wealthier parts of the city but continue to operate in its poorer neighbourhoods. Legislation to phase out the industry was passed in 2022.

7 Harry's line is: 'Men and women can't be *friends* because the *sex* part always gets in the way'.

8 In the Spanish DVD of the film this return is even more emphatic. The scene in which Carolina acknowledges to Albert that his is 'the face' of her 'perfect guy' is missing, so that Albert's final appearance and speech seem unequivocally one of a claim to ownership despite Carolina's own misgivings.

9 Kirov was Secretary of the Central Committee of the Communist Party. His assassination in Leningrad was used as justification for Stalin's purges of the following years.

10 The passage closes the final chapter of Part One, and concludes: 'for you are overtaking the whole world, and shall one day force all nations, all empires to stand aside, to give you way!'

11 This is also true of other poets quoted in the film. Mandelstam died in a transit camp of typhoid fever in 1938. Tsvetaeva died by suicide in 1941 after the execution of her husband.

12 Article 58, which had many sub-clauses, was put in place in 1927 to prosecute those suspected of counter-revolutionary activities.

13 See Denise Riley: 'because that usual intuition of flowing time has been halted, narration itself can't proceed. ... Your very condition militates against narrative' ([2012] 2020: 108).

14 The novel is a social critique by Ivan Goncharov, published in 1859.

15 The poem was originally published in Russian in Mandelstam's collection *Stone* in 1909. The translation used in the film can be found in Schmidt 2007.

Conclusion: other stories

When I began this book Marleen Gorris's first three films were almost unavailable: *A Question of Silence* and *The Last Island* could be watched only via YouTube uploads of digitised VHS copies; *Broken Mirrors* could be watched via Learning on Screen's Box of Broadcasts, uploaded from a 1990 screening on Channel 4 which came complete with a content warning for this 'disturbingly powerful thriller'. The 2023 restoration and re-issue of the films on DVD by Cult Epics has changed this, so that these films can be watched afresh, and the continuities which I have attempted to trace through Gorris's nearly thirty-year filmmaking career can now be more easily considered by others. In her booklet accompanying the first pressing of what Cult Epics calls 'the Marleen Gorris trilogy', Anneke Smelik, the most consistent champion of Gorris's films throughout this period, writes of their origins in the activism of 1970s second wave feminism, when feminist directors, like feminist novelists and feminist artists, began to tell stories which focused not simply on women's victimisation, but more importantly on their 'resistance to sexism, male violence and social injustice' (2023: 4). Gorris's early films, she continues, had an enormous impact within the communities of the Women's Movement, making women like Smelik herself 'feel visible for the first time' (ibid.), but she adds that their stories of resistance are no less relevant today. The resistance of which Smelik writes is political, and in insisting on its continued relevance she has in mind recent collective movements like #MeToo which, in seeking to fight sexism, harassment and sexual violence, 'revisits many of those earlier feminist themes' (ibid.). This book has sought to consider it in rather different, more theoretical terms, where resistance has been reimagined in relation to ideas of vulnerability and a relationally constituted self, and to the rethinking of time and space that such a theorisation implies.

Stories

Gorris, writes Smelik in her 2023 booklet, 'can be considered a realist filmmaker, . . . a storyteller [who] chose to tell her feminist stories in a combination of conventional genres' (2023: 3–4). She is drawing here on a 1990 interview she conducted with Gorris, where the filmmaker reflects on the nature of her storytelling. 'For me', she says, 'the story as a narrative form does not exclude the possibility of political content. . . . I can't connect with experimental films. . . . they don't capture my imagination'. She continues:

> I find storytelling to be one of the most interesting ways to convey something. Traditionally that's how it has always been. Stories were passed down from generation to generation. When I make a film, I want people to be there in the cinema, not driven away, so I have to come up with something that will keep them engaged for at least that hour and a half. That, for me, is the story. But I don't mean just that a story has to have a beginning, a middle and an end, but that there must be something interwoven within it . . . Most films aim for identification with a person: is that man nice or not nice and what does he do, what doesn't he do? I've noticed that I always look for identification with the *problem*. And that is something quite different. The medium for the problem, the person who does something, must of course be understandable and relatable. But for me it is primarily about the situation,[1] how that situation develops and how people deal with it. What the film is about is the most important thing to me [though] it must be embodied successfully by the actors, because as a viewer you have to go along with them, you can't give up halfway. (Smelik 1990: 247)

I have quoted the interview at length because it touches on a number of the themes of this book. At this early stage of her career, Gorris is clear in positioning herself against the influential arguments that had been made by feminist film theorists like Laura Mulvey (1979) and the *Camera Obscura* collective (1976), that feminist content must be matched by an experimental form if a feminist (counter-)cinema was to emerge. She is concerned, she says, with stories, and with the traditional forms in which they have been told. But whilst this would seem to imply a linear temporal structure and identification with a single protagonist who moves through this structure towards resolution and the establishment of meaning, she is equally clear that this is not her concern. It is the problem, or situation, and how this might be confronted that is her focus, though this working through must be embodied in characters who are intelligible ('understandable') and relatable.

To focus on the problem or situation is to resist what Margaret Homans calls 'the illusion of progress powerfully suggested by sequence' (1994: 5). It is to still the forward movement of narrative, to move away from what narratologist Gérard Genette calls its 'temporal, dramatic aspect' and towards that which 'suspend[s] the course of time and . . . contribute[s] to spreading the narrative in space' (1982: 136–7). It is this suspended time that Lisa Baraitser identifies with time 'lived *in the feminine*' (2017: 79; her emphasis), and with forms of resistance linked with vulnerability, care and community. To make this move whilst working with established narrative forms and genres, and with characters who remain intelligible and empathetic, involves finding ways of interrupting, disrupting and making visible the generic structures within which the filmmaker is working, and which provide, as Lauren Berlant argues (2011a: 176), the normative frameworks which render us, as gendered subjects, socially intelligible. Gorris's films, I have suggested, are concerned to explore the possibilities of resistance within normative structures, both social and generic, imagined most often through a marginalised and abjected community of women, and some men, whose subjects are marked by vulnerability (corporeal, economic, political) but also by care and agency. If the *problem* she confronts is how this resistance might be imagined, and lived, within or in relation to the historical world as we know it, and within generic structures that function to reaffirm its norms, it is a problem that is played out across a range of different *situations,* from the mythical to the generically conventional.

And genres

Gorris's earliest films, where, as she says, she 'never had to make concessions, and . . . had the final cut' (2023), are her most radical and aesthetically adventurous. Here she plays with, cites, inverts and disrupts generic conventions, whilst also suggesting the possibility of another story, one built upon the different lived, liveable and fantasised times of women's experience. At times this emerges through temporal shifts and breaks, in fragmentary sequences which interrupt the forward narrative movement; at times it is embodied in the rhythms and repetitions, the jokes and expressions of care, in the daily lives of a community of women; at times it is no more than an attenuated hope for the future. In *Antonia's Line* it receives its fullest expression, in an alternative, matriarchal space–time, in which the nascent, fragile and marginal communities of women pictured in Gorris's first two films and the half-suggested female genealogy glimpsed at the end of *The Last Island* are fully realised and celebrated, and the temporal and spatial possibilities of cinematic narrative reimagined.

Gorris's move into mainstream filmmaking following the Oscar success of *Antonia's Line* saw her working within the 'feminine' genres of literary adaptation/heritage film and romcom, from scripts produced by others and within imposed production constraints. It was a move that gave her far more limited opportunities to realise her vision of a resistance grounded in a women-centred community, with its foregrounding of other possible temporalities and relationships. Both of her literary adaptations use the visual patterns and social rituals of the heritage film to emphasise restriction. Their worlds are as patriarchal as that which she depicts in her first two films, and their female protagonists must survive in a world in which, as in *Antonia's Line*, war and patriarchy are indissolubly linked. Unlike in *Antonia's Line*, however, that world is now oppressively central within the films and the women within it isolated. Only moments of other possible stories, temporalities and relationships are glimpsed in *Mrs Dalloway*, though the radical reimagining of Nabokov's novel in *The Luzhin Defence*, with its female protagonist and rewritten ending, does, particularly in its 'What if' final act, point us outwards from its restricted world towards those possibilities. In *Carolina*, the matriarchal world of *Antonia's Line*, with its temporality of seasons and generations, its rhythms of the body and of the ebbs and flows of community, returns as a source of resistance, this time pitted against the narrative structure of the contemporary romantic comedy and its post-feminist logic. The film's compromises are, however, uneasy, its two narrative worlds at odds.

As her most fully realised authorial vision, *Antonia's Line* addresses Gorris's themes most directly and articulates most fully the tropes through which it is imagined. It engages with the idea of myth, with the power of stories and genres, and it meditates explicitly on time. It evokes the art of painting to arrest narrative progression and expand the suspended moment, but also reflects on the power structures art embodies. It conjures another space of possibility, inclusive, generous and matriarchal, but reminds us always of the presence, at the edge of our frame of vision, of state oppression and patriarchal power, and of the line of continuity between those structures and individual acts of brutality. It is polyvocal, providing a sense of multiple, cross-generational authorship for its story. It is the product, writes Kathleen Rowe Karlyn (2011) of a 'wicked powerful feminism' which centres life: 'Life's got to be lived', says Antonia, for 'this is the only dance we dance'. Its celebration is embodied in communal feasts, and in the corporeal pleasures of sex and, as Antonia suggests, dance, for if both of these can be used to display the gendered power structures of a patriarchal society, as Gorris shows elsewhere, they can also subvert them, suspending linear time in the shared pleasures of the body.

Gorris's last film, *Within the Whirlwind*, returns powerfully to these themes, now in the context of a historically specific space and time – Kristeva's 'time of project and history' ([1979] 1986a: 193) – not the transformed space-time of *Antonia's Line*. In adapting a memoir, too, it takes on a genre traditionally centred on the individual, in which, in Annette Kuhn's words, the narrating 'I' constructs and makes public 'a certain self, a particular identity' (2000: 180) through the power of its authorial voice. For the memoir's author Eugenia Ginzburg, this individual journey of suffering in Stalin's labour camps was towards her own moral and political understanding, and in narrating it she consciously places herself within a tradition of classic Russian literature. In Gorris's film, however, we find a community of women at its centre. In her account of women's role within narratives of imperial conquest, Anne McClintock writes that in them women 'are relegated to a realm beyond history' (1995: 31), often within 'abject zones' occupied by groups who are expelled and 'obliged to inhabit the impossible edges of modernity' (ibid.: 72). The abject space of the Gulag camps is one such zone, but if it is characterised by brutality, vulnerability and loss, it is also a space in which time's suspension – modes of enduring, waiting, persisting – gives rise to practices of care which become a resistance grounded in the shared recognition of that vulnerability. Gorris uses poetry here as she used painting in *Antonia's Line* to create a sense of the expanded suspended moment and a shared narrative voice, and as there she creates rhythms of repetition and slow, seasonal change.

Other stories

Like *A Question of Silence* and *The Luzhin Defence*, *Within the Whirlwind* ends on a freeze-frame of a woman's face looking out at and beyond us, inviting us, as *Antonia's Line* does more explicitly, to continue the story. Gorris herself has not made another film, however, and this fact points to an alternative narrative around which this book might have been organised and which has been present as a kind of shadow narrative throughout. The marginalisation of women within the film industry has been highlighted by a number of studies (Cobb et al 2018, Eikhof et al. 2018, Follows et al. 2016, Hunt et al. 2019, Smith et al. 2019). Summarising such findings, Natalie Wreyford and Shelley Cobb conclude that 'according to the data, the main plot of the twenty-first-century history of women's filmmaking so far is one of pervasive absence and exclusion' (2017: 124). Marleen Gorris's own filmmaking history includes the collapse of the production company for one of her films, First Floor Features, and with it the disappearance of *The Last Island,* a film finally restored from a single remaining copy. It involves, too, distribution failures: 'Most of the distributors were men at that time', she writes, and would have been hostile to her early films. 'In those days', she continues, 'there was never any consultation between the producer and me about distribution. I never knew when and to which countries and for how much my films were sold. If I asked, I was probably lied to' (2023). It includes, too, producer-made changes and deletions to a completed film (*Carolina*), and the disappearance of promised finance during the filming schedule, as well as a producer who refused to pay part of her salary. Gorris's final proposed film was called off two days before shooting was to begin. 'Over the years', she says, 'it became increasing difficult to get films made, both abroad and in Holland, probably not least because I'm a woman and a feminist' (ibid.). In trying to make them, she reflects, it was not 'irate critics' that were the greatest impediment, but the difficult and at times hostile production and distribution structure.

This is, as I said, a shadow narrative in this book, which has sought instead to foreground the vision embodied in Gorris's films, and the means through which this is articulated. This vision, which she describes as centring on 'the survival of women in a patriarchal world' (Gorris 2023), is not, of course, separate from her own thirty-year struggle to keep making films. In celebrating it I am aware that I am, in the words of Shelley Cobb and Yvonne Tasker (2016), offering 'a political as well as aesthetic response' to a body of films that themselves speak always to what Cobb and Tasker, in their review of 'Feminist Film Criticism in the 21st Century', call 'the scandal of women's marginalization'.[2] The films of Marleen Gorris, however, demonstrate clearly that these two responses are not separate. To trace the revisioning of narrative, time and space in her films, and her vision of the possibilities of other narratives, other subjectivities and other relationships, is also to trace the history of a powerful feminist resistance to the structural constraints, both social and generic, against which that vision was realised.

Notes

1   The original interview is in Dutch. In the 2023 audio commentary for *The Last Island*, Peter Verstraten provides a translation, and it is this translation that I have largely used here. Gorris, however, talks of her films revolving around a 'gegeven', literally a 'given'. Verstraten translates this as 'concept', but I have preferred 'situation'. Gorris herself comments that the term is difficult to translate: 'It seems to be a bit of everything: situation, concept, a given, subject', but would prefer 'situation' (2024).

2   They write:

> when engaged through a feminist perspective, film criticism notices the scandal of women's marginalization. It responds to that marginalization in multiple ways – in detail, in outline, through engagement with history or writing about the contemporary moment. Motivated by an understanding of inequality and an interest in cinema, feminist film criticism offers a political as well as aesthetic response to visual culture.

Bibliography

Ackroyd, Peter (1984), 'Dressing Up', *Spectator* April 14.

Adam, Barbara (1995), *Timewatch*, Cambridge: Polity Press.

Alexandrov, Vladimir E. (1991), *Nabokov's Otherworld*, Princeton: Princeton University Press.

Bainbridge, Caroline (2008), *A Feminine Cinematics: Luce Irigaray, Women and Film*, Houndmills: Palgrave Macmillan.

Bakhtin, Mikhail ([1965] 1994a/), 'Folk Humour and Carnival Laughter', in Pam Morris (ed.), *The Bakhtin Reader*, London: Arnold, pp. 194–206.

Bakhtin, Mikhail ([1965] 1994b), 'Carnival Ambivalence: Laughter, Praise and Abuse', in Pam Morris (ed.), *The Bakhtin Reader*, London: Arnold, pp. 206–26.

Ballantyne, R. M. (Robert Michael) ([1858] 1994), *The Coral Island*, Puffin Classics, Harmondsworth: Penguin.

Baraitser, Lisa (2009), *Maternal Encounters*, London and New York: Routledge.

Baraitser, Lisa (2017), *Enduring Time*, London: Bloomsbury Academic.

Baraitser, Lisa, and Denise Riley (2016), 'Lisa Baraitser in Conversation with Denise Riley', *Studies in the Maternal* 8.1: 1–16.

Bell, Vereen (2006), 'Misreading *Mrs. Dalloway*', *The Sewanee Review* 114.1: 93–111.

Berlant, Lauren (1988), 'The Female Complaint', *Social Text* 19/20: 237–59.

Berlant, Lauren (1998), 'Intimacy', *Critical Inquiry* 24.2: 281–8.

Berlant, Lauren (2008), *The Female Complaint*, Durham, NC, and London: Duke University Press.

Berlant, Lauren (2011a), *Cruel Optimism*, Durham, NC: Duke University Press.

Berlant, Lauren (2011b), (November), 'Austerity, Precarity, Awkwardness'. Last accessed 10 October 2024, at: https://supervalentthought.files. wordpress.com/2011/12/berlant-aaa-2011final.pdf.

Blackwelder, Rob (2001), '"Luzhin" Something in the Translation', *Spliced Wire* April 27. Last accessed 10 October 2024, at: http://splicedwire.com/ 01reviews/luzhin.html.

Bluestone, George ([1957] 1968), *Novels into Film,* Berkeley and Los Angeles: University of California Press.

Bovkis, Elen A. (1997), 'The Magical World of the Ultimate Matriarch', *Cineaction* 43: 50–7.

Boyd, Brian (1987), 'The Problem of Pattern: Nabokov's "Defense"', *Modern Fiction Studies* 33.4: 575–604.

Bracke, Sarah (2016), 'Bouncing Back: Vulnerability and Resistance in Times of Resilience', in Judith Butler, Zeynep Gambetti and Leticia Sabsay (eds.), *Vulnerability in Resistance,* Durham, NC, and London: Duke University Press, pp. 52–75.

Browne, Victoria (2014), *Feminism, Time, and Nonlinear History.* New York: Palgrave Macmillan.

Bufkin, E. C. (1965), '*Lord of the Flies*: An Analysis', *The Georgia Review* 19.1: 40–57.

Butler, Judith (1994), '"Feminism by Any Other Name"; Interview with Rosi Braidotti', *Differences: A Journal of Feminist Cultural Studies* 6.2–3: 27–61.

Butler, Judith (1997), *The Psychic Life of Power,* Stanford: Stanford University Press.

Butler, Judith (2004a), *Precarious Life,* London and New York: Verso.

Butler, Judith (2004b), *Undoing Gender,* New York: Routledge.

Butler, Judith (2005), *Giving an Account of Oneself,* New York: Fordham University Press.

Butler, Judith (2014), 'On Cruelty', *London Review of Books* 36.14: 31–3.

Butler, Judith (2016), 'Rethinking Vulnerability and Resistance', in Judith Butler, Zeynep Gambetti and Leticia Sabsay (eds.), *Vulnerability in Resistance,* Durham, NC, and London: Duke University Press, pp. 12–27.

Butler, Judith, Zeynep Gambetti, and Leticia Sabsay (eds.) (2016), 'Introduction', in Judith Butler, Zeynep Gambetti and Leticia Sabsay (eds.), *Vulnerability in Resistance,* Durham, NC and London: Duke University Press, pp. 1–11.

Butler, Judith (2019), 'Out of Breath: Laughing, Crying at the Body's Limit', lecture at The Hemispheric Institute, New York University, 5 August. Last accessed 21 October 2024, at: https://hemisphericinstitute.org/en/encuentro-2019-keynote-lectures/item/3084-keynote-lectures-004.html.

Camera Obscura collective (1976), 'Feminism and Film: Critical Approaches', *Camera Obscura* 1: 1–10.

Campbell, Joseph ([1949] 1993), *The Hero with a Thousand Faces,* London: Fontana.

Castell, David (1983), 'The Power and the Crystal', *Sunday Telegraph* 20 February, p. 14.

Cavarero, Adriana (2000), *Relating Narratives,* trans. with introduction by Paul A. Kottman, London and New York: Routledge.

Cavarero Adriana, with Elisabetta Bertolino (2008), 'Beyond Ontology and Sexual Difference: An Interview with the Italian Feminist Philosopher Adriana Cavarero', *Differences* 19.1: 128–67.

Cawelti, John G. (1997), 'Canonization, Modern Literature, and the Detective Story', in Jerome H. Delamater and Ruth Prigozy (eds.), *Theory and Practice of Classic Detective Fiction*, Westport, CT, and London: Greenwood Press, pp. 5–15.

Chatman, Seymour (1981), 'What Novels Can Do that Films Can't (and Vice Versa)', in W. J. T. Mitchell (ed) *On Narrative*, Chicago and London: University of Chicago Press, pp. 117–36.

Chodorow, Nancy (1978), *The Reproduction of Mothering*, Berkeley, Los Angeles, London: University of California Press.

Christie, Ian (1978), 'The Scandal of *Peeping Tom*', in Ian Christie (ed.), *Powell, Pressburger and Others*, London: BFI, pp. 53–8.

Citron, Michelle (1988), 'Women's Film Production: Going Mainstream', in E. Deidre Pribram (ed.), *Female Spectators*, London: Verso, pp. 45–63.

Cixous, Hélène (1980), 'The Laugh of the Medusa' trans. Keith Cohen and Paula Cohen, in Elaine Marks and Isabelle de Courtivron (eds.), *New French Feminisms*, Brighton: Harvester, pp. 245–64.

Clover, Carol J. (1992), *Men, Women, and Chain Saws*, London: BFI.

Cobb, Shelley, Linda Ruth Williams and Natalie Wreyford (2018), *Women Directors and Cinematographers*. Last accessed 21 October 2024, at: https://womencallingtheshots.com/reports-and-publications/.

Cobb, Shelley and Yvonne Tasker (2016), 'Feminist Film Criticism in the 21st Century', *Film Criticism* 40.1. Last accessed 21 October 2024, at DOI: https://doi.org/10.3998/fc.13761232.0040.107.

Coleridge, Samuel Taylor ([1798] 2000), *The Rime of the Ancient Mariner*, New York: Dover Publications.

Conrad, Joseph ([1899] 2007), *Heart of Darkness*, Penguin Classics, Harmondsworth: Penguin.

Cook, Pam (1985), Review of *Broken Mirrors (Gebroken Spiegels)*, *Monthly Film Bulletin* 52.612: 113–4.

Cook, Richard (1982), Review of *A Question of Silence*, *New Musical Express* 4 December, p. 26.

Cooke, Olga M. (ed.) (2023a), *A Mind Purified by Suffering: Evgenia Ginzburg's "Whirlwind" Memoirs*, Boston: Academic Studies Press.

Cooke, Olga M. (2023b), 'Introduction', in Olga M. Cooke (ed.), *A Mind Purified by Suffering: Evgenia Ginzburg's "Whirlwind" Memoirs*, Boston: Academic Studies Press, pp. xiii–xxxii.

Cuddy-Keane, Melba (1998), 'Mrs. Dalloway: Film, Time, and Trauma', in Laura Davisand Jeanette McVicker (eds.), *Virginia Woolf and Her Influences: Selected Papers from the Seventh Annual Conference on Virginia Woolf*, New York: Pace University Press, pp. 171–5.

Culler, Jonathan (2001), *The Pursuit of Signs*, London: Routledge.

Curti, Lidia (1988), 'Genre and Gender', *Cultural Studies* 2.2: 152–67.

Davies, Karen (1990), *Women, Time and the Weaving of the Strands of Everyday Life*, Aldershot: Avebury.

De Lauretis, Teresa (1984), *Alice Doesn't: Feminism, Semiotics, Cinema*, Basingstoke and London: Macmillan.

Defoe, Daniel ([1719a] 2012), *The Strange and Surprising Adventures of Robinson Crusoe*, New York: Dover Publications.

Defoe, Daniel (1719b), *The Farther Adventures of Robinson Crusoe*, London: W. Taylor.

Delacoste, Frédérique and Felice Newman (eds.) (1981), *Fight Back! Feminist Resistance to Male Violence*, New Jersey: Cleis Press.

Deleyto, Celestino (2009), *The Secret Life of Romantic Comedy*, Manchester and New York: Manchester University Press.

Denby, David (1998), 'Grace Notes', *New York Magazine* February 23. Last accessed 21 October 2024, at: https://nymag.com/nymetro/movies/reviews/2260/.

Diamond, Irene and Lee Quinby (eds.) (1988), *Feminism and Foucault: Reflections on Resistance*, Boston: Northeastern University Press.

Dittmar, Linda (1986), 'Beyond Gender and Within It: The Social Construction of Female Desire', *Wide Angle* 8.4: 79–88.

Doane, Mary Ann (1987) *The Desire to Desire*, Basingstoke: Macmillan Press.

Doane, Mary Ann ([1982] 1991), 'Film and the Masquerade: Theorising the Female Spectator', in Mary Ann Doane, *Femmes Fatales: Feminism, Film Theory, Psychoanalysis*, New York and London: Routledge, pp. 17–32.

Doane, Mary Ann (2002), *The Emergence of Cinematic Time*, Cambridge and London: Harvard University Press.

DuPlessis, Rachel Blau (1985), *Writing Beyond the Ending*, Bloomington: Indiana University Press.

Ebert, Roger (1998), Review of *Mrs Dalloway*, *Chicago Sun-Times* March 6. Last accessed 21 October 2024, at: https://www.rogerebert.com/reviews/mrs-dalloway-1998.

Eikhof, Doris Ruth, Jack Newsinger, Daria Luchinskaya and Daniela Aidley (2018), 'And … Action? Gender, Knowledge and Inequalities in the Screen Industries', *Gender Work Organ* 26.6: 840–59.

Ellis, Joan (1998), '*Mrs Dalloway* Review', *Illusion*. Last accessed 21 October 2024, at: https://joanellis.com/reviews/MRS._DALLOWAY.htm.

Ermarth, Elizabeth Deeds (1989), 'The Solitude of Women and Social Time', in Frieda Johles Forman with Caoran Sowton (eds.), *Taking our Time*, Oxford and New York: Pergamon Press, pp. 37–46.

Ermarth, Elizabeth Deeds (1998), *Realism and Consensus in the English Novel*, Edinburgh: Edinburgh University Press.

Faith, Karen (1994), 'Resistance: Lessons from Foucault and Feminism', in H. Lorraine Radtke and Henderikus J. Stam (eds.), *Power/Gender: Social Relations in Theory and Practice,* London: Sage, pp. 36–66.

Felski, Rita (2000), *Doing Time,* New York and London: New York University Press.

Fischer, Lucy (1989), 'Murder, She Wrote: Women who Kill', in Fischer, *Shot/Countershot,* Princeton: Princeton University Press, pp. 269–300.

Fiske, John (1987), *Television Culture,* London: Methuen.

Follows, Stephen, Alexis Kreager and Eleanor Gomes (2016), *Cut Out of the Picture: A Study of Gender Inequality Among Film Directors Within in the UK Film Industry.* Last accessed 21 October 2024, at https://www.directors.uk.com/news/cut-out-of-the-picture.

French, Philip (1983), 'All in the Mind', *The Observer* 20 February, p. 30.

French, Philip (2000), 'Grandmaster Crash', *The Guardian* September 10. Last accessed 21 October 2024, at: https://www.theguardian.com/film/2000/sep/10/chess.philipfrench.

Friedman, Susan Stanford (1989), 'Lyric Subversion of Narrative in Women's Writing: Virginia Woolf and the Tyranny of Plot', in James Phelan (ed.), *Reading Narrative: Form, Ethics, Ideology.* Columbus: Ohio State University Press, pp. 162–85.

Frye, Northrop (1957), *Anatomy of Criticism: Four Essays.* Princeton: Princeton University Press.

Frye, Northrop (1976), *The Secular Scripture: A Study of the Structure of Romance,* Cambridge, MA, and London: Harvard University Press.

Gallo, Bill (2001), Review of *The Luzhin Defence, Miami New Times* April 19. Last accessed 21 October 2024, at: https://www.rottentomatoes.com/m/the_luzhin_defence/reviews.

Genette, Gérard (1982), *Figures of Literary Discourse,* trans. Alan Sheridan, Oxford: Blackwell.

Gentile, Mary C. ([1985] 1991), 'Feminist or Tendentious? Marleen Gorris's *A Question of Silence*', in Patricia Erens (ed.), *Issues in Feminist Film Criticism,* Bloomington and Indianapolis: Indiana University Press, pp. 395–404.

Geraghty, Christine (2008), *Now a Major Motion Picture,* Lanham, MD: Rowman & Littlefield.

Gill, Rosalind and Shani Orgad (2017), 'Confidence Culture and the Remaking of Feminism', *New Formations* 91: 16–34.

Gill, Rosalind and Shani Orgad (2018), 'The Amazing Bounce-Backable Woman: Resilience and the Psychological Turn in Neoliberalism', *Sociological Research Online* 23.2: 477–95.

Gilligan, Carol (1982), *In a Different Voice,* Cambridge, MA: Harvard University Press.

Ginzburg, Eugenia Semyonovna (1967), *Journey into the Whirlwind*, trans. Paul Stevenson and Max Hayward, San Diego, New York, London: Harcourt Brace Jovanovich.

Ginzburg, Eugenia Semyonovna (1981), *Within the Whirlwind*, trans. Ian Boland, New York: Harcourt Brace Jovanovich.

Gogol, Nikolay ([1842] 2004), *Dead Souls*, trans. Robert Maguire, London: Penguin Books.

Golding, William *Lord of the Flies* ([1954] 2012), London: Faber and Faber.

Gonchorov, Ivan ([1859] 2005), *Oblomov*, trans. David Magarshack, with an introduction by Milton Ehre, Harmondsworth: Penguin.

Gorris, Marleen (1990), *Het Nederlands Scenario* 3 ('Drie scenarios van Marleen Gorris'), Amsterdam: International Theatre and Film Books.

Gorris, Marleen (2023), personal communication, July.

Gorris, Marleen (2024), personal communication, July.

Gorton, Kristyn (2021), '"Don't Let the Bastards Grind You Down": Feminist Resilience/Resilient Feminism in *The Handmaid's Tale* (Hulu, 2017–)', *Critical Studies in Television* 16.3: 227–44.

Greven, David (2011), *Representations of Femininity in American Genre Cinema*, New York: Palgrave Macmillan.

Groom, Amelia (2022), 'Eruptions of Silence: The Unheard, the Unsaid, and the Politics of Laughter in Marleen Gorris's *A Question of Silence*', *Another Screen*. Last accessed 21 October 2024, at: https://www.another-screen.com/silence-laughter.

Guthmann, Edward (1998), 'Redgrave Makes Best of Tedious "Dalloway"', *SFGate* March 6. Last accessed 21 October 2024, at: https://www.sfgate.com/movies/article/Redgrave-Makes-Best-Of-Tedious-Dalloway-3012166.php.

Hagelin, Sarah (2013), *Reel Vulnerability: Power, Pain, and Gender in Contemporary American Film and Television*, New Brunswick: Rutgers University Press.

Hall, Stuart and Tony Jefferson (eds.) (1976), *Resistance Through Rituals: Youth Subcultures in Post-War Britain*, London: HarperCollins.

Hankins, Leslie Kathleen (1999), '"Colour Burning on a Framework of Steel": Virginia Woolf, Marleen Gorris, Eileen Atkins, and Mrs. Dalloway', *Women's Studies: An Interdisciplinary Journal*, 28.4: 367–77.

Hemmings, Clare (2011), *Why Stories Matter*, Durham, NC, and London: Duke University Press.

Higgins, Lesley and Marie-Christine Leps (2000), '*Mrs Dalloway* and *Orlando*: The Subject of Time and Generic Transactions', in Deborah Cartmell, I. Q. Hunter, Heidi Kaye and Imelda Whelehan (eds.), *Classics in Film and Fiction*, London: Pluto, pp. 116–36.

Higson, Andrew (1993), 'Re-presenting the National Past: Nostalgia and Pastiche in the Heritage Film', in Lester Friedman (ed.), *British Cinema and Thatcherism*, London: UCL Press, pp. 109–29.

Higson, Andrew (1996), 'The Heritage Film and British Cinema', in Andrew Higson (ed.), *Dissolving Views: Key Writings on British Cinema*, London: Cassell, pp. 232–48.

Higson, Andrew (2003), *English Heritage, English Cinema*, Oxford: Oxford University Press.

Hinxman, Margaret (1983), 'So Little Fun in Fairyland', *Daily Mail* 18 February, p. 23.

Hirsch, Marianne (1989), *The Mother/Daughter Plot*, Bloomington and Indianapolis: Indiana University Press.

Hirsch, Marianne (2016), 'Vulnerable Times', in Judith Butler, Zeynep Gambetti and Leticia Sabsay (eds.), *Vulnerability in Resistance*, Durham, NC, and London: Duke University Press, pp. 76–96.

Homans, Margaret (1994), 'Feminist Fictions and Feminist Theories of Narrative', *Narrative* 2.1: 3–16.

Honkasalo, Marja-Liisa (2018), 'Introduction: Vulnerability and Inquiring into Relationality', *The Finnish Journal of Social Anthropology* 43.3: 1–21.

Hunt, Darnell, Ana-Christina Ramón, and Michael Tran (2019), *Hollywood Diversity Report: 2019*. UCLA Social Sciences. Last accessed 21 October 2024, at https://socialsciences.ucla.edu/wp-content/uploads/2024/06/UCLA-Hollywood-Diversity-Report-2019-2-21-2019.pdf.

Hunter, Stephen (2001), 'Checkmate: The Cast in Unconventionally Played "Luzhin Defence" Is Well Matched', *Washington Post* May 4. Last accessed 10 October 2024, at: https://www.washingtonpost.com/wp-srv/entertainment/movies/reviews/theluzhindefencehunter.htm.

Ingersoll, Earl G. (2017), *Screening Woolf: Virginia Woolf on/and/in Film*, Madison, Fairleigh Dickinson University Press.

Ingold, Tim (1993), 'The Temporality of the Landscape', *World Archaeology* 25.2: 152–74.

Jackson, Virginia (2015), 'The Function of Criticism at the Present Time', *Los Angeles Review of Books* special series "No Crisis", April 12. Last accessed 10 October 2024, at: https://lareviewofbooks.org/article/function-criticism-present-time/.

Jaehne, Karen (1996), '*Antonia's Line*', *Film Quarterly*, 50.1: 27–30.

Jeffords, Susan (1994), *Hard Bodies: Hollywood Masculinity in the Reagan Era*, New Brunswick: Rutgers University Press.

Johnston, Sheila (1983), '*A Question of Silence (De Stilte Rond Christine M)*', *Monthly Film Bulletin*; 50.588: 48.

Kelly, Catriona (1994), *A History of Russian Women's Writing 1820–1992*, Oxford: Clarendon Press.

Keough, Peter (1998), Review *Mrs Dalloway, Boston Phoenix* March 5. Last accessed 10 October 2024, at: https://bostonphoenix.com/archives/1998/documents/00524968.htm.

Kermode, Mark (2023), 'Women Talking' Review, *Observer* 12 February. Last accessed 10 October 2024, at: https://www.theguardian.com/film/2023/feb/12/women-talking-review-sarah-polley-timeless-parable-sexual-abuse-mennonites-rooney-mara-claire-foy-jessie-buckley-frances-mcdormand.

Koivunen, Anu, Katariina Kyrölä and Ingrid Ryberg (2018), 'Vulnerability as a Political Language', in Anu Koivunen, Katariina Kyrölä and Ingrid Ryberg (eds.), *The Power of Vulnerability*, Manchester: Manchester University Press, pp. 1–26.

Krabbé, Tim (2001), 'Nabokov as a Feminist', *Open Chess Diary 101–120* (10 March – 30 May), 103 (22 March). Last accessed 10 October 2024, at: https://timkr.home.xs4all.nl/chess2/diary_6.htm.

Kristeva, Julia ([1979] 1986a), 'Women's Time', trans. Alice Jardine and Harry Blake in Toril Moi (ed.), *The Kristeva Reader*, Oxford: Blackwell, pp. 188–213.

Kristeva, Julia ([1977] 1986b), 'A New Type of Intellectual: The Dissident', trans. Hand, Seán, in Toril Moi (ed.), *The Kristeva Reader*, Oxford: Blackwell, pp. 292–300.

Kroll, Jack (1998), 'Down in the Upper Crust: Virginia Woolf's Landmark Novel Dazzles on Screen'. *Newsweek* March 2, p. 80.

Kruger, Barbara (1983), '*A Question of Silence*', *Artforum* 21.10, p. 83.

Krutnik, Frank (2002), 'Conforming Passions? Contemporary Romantic Comedy', in Steve Neale (ed.), *Genre and Contemporary Hollywood*, London: BFI Publishing, pp. 130–47.

Kuhn, Annette (2000), A Journey Through Memory'. In Susannah Radstone (ed.) *Memory and Methodology*. Oxford: Berg, pp. 179–96.

Lawrence, D. H. ([1926] 2007), 'The Rocking Horse Winner', in Sue Wilson (ed.), *D. H. Lawrence Selected Stories*, London: Penguin, pp. 269–85.

Lawrence, D. H. (1960), *Lady Chatterley's Lover*, Harmondsworth: Penguin.

Lefanu, Sarah (1983), 'A Matter of Murder', *Time Out* 18–24 February.

Levy, Emanuel (1996), 'A Fairy Tale', *The Advocate*, 5 March, pp. 64–5.

Linthorst, Gerdin (1996), 'Marleen Gorris, a Feminist Moralist', *Our Heritage/Ons Erfdeel*, 39.1: 191–200.

Loxley, Diana (1990), *Problematic Shores: The Literature of Islands*, New York: Palgrave Macmillan.

Mackintosh, Helen (1983), 'Asking Why', *City Limits* 18–24 February, p. 20.

Maio, Kathi (1996), 'Antonia, Anne . . . and Oscar', *On the Issues* 5.3: 54–5.

Marcus, Jane (1994), 'Registering Objections: Grounding Feminist Alibis', in Margaret R. Higonnet, and Joan Templeton (eds.), *Reconfigured Spheres:*

Feminist Explorations of Literary Space, Amherst: University of Massachusetts Press, pp. 171–93.

Maslin, Janet (1983), 'Silence of Killers', *New York Times* 18 March, p. 132.

Maslin, Janet (1996), 'Film Review: A Line of Strong Women with Faith in Destiny', *New York Times* 2 February, p. 18.

Maslin, Janet (1998), 'Truths of all Lives, Comfortable or Not: Virginia Woolf's *Mrs Dalloway*', *New York Times* February 20, p. E12.

Mazierska, Ewa (2011), *Nabokov's Cinematic Afterlife*, London: McFarland & Co.

McClintock, Anne (1995), *Imperial Leather: Race, Gender and Sexuality in the Colonial Contest*, New York and London: Routledge.

McNay, Lois (1992), *Foucault and Feminism*, Cambridge: Polity.

McRobbie, Angela and Jenny Garber (1976), 'Girls and Subcultures: An Exploration', in Stuart Hall and Tony Jefferson (eds.), *Resistance through Rituals: Youth Subcultures in Post-War Britain*, London: HarperCollins, pp. 209–22.

McRobbie, Angela (2020), *Feminism and the Politics of 'Resilience': Essays on Gender, Media and the End of Welfare*, London: Polity.

Miracky, James (2001), 'A Simultaneous Flow: Diachronic, Psychological, and Synchronic Time in the Novel and Film Versions of *Mrs Dalloway*', *Interfaces. Image-Texte-Langage* 19–20: 225–40.

Mitchell, W. J. T. (1984), 'The Politics of Genre: Space and Time in Lessing's *Laocoon*', *Representations* 6 (Spring): 98–115.

Modleski, Tania (1987), 'Time and Desire in the Woman's Film', in Christine Gledhill (ed.), *Home is Where the Heart is: Studies in Melodrama and the Woman's Film*, London: B.F.I. pp. 326–38.

Moi, Toril (1986), 'Introduction to "'Women's Time'", in Toril Moi (ed.), *The Kristeva Reader*, Oxford: Blackwell, pp. 187–8.

Monk, Claire (1998), Review of *Mrs Dalloway*, *Sight and Sound* March, 8.3: 53.

Morgan, Monique (2009) *Narrative Means, Lyric Ends*, Columbus: Ohio State University Press.

Mortimer, Claire (2010), *Romantic Comedy*, London and New York: Routledge.

Mulvey, Laura ([1975] 2009), 'Visual Pleasure and Narrative Cinema', in Laura Mulvey, *Visual and Other Pleasures*, second edn, Basingstoke and London: Palgrave Macmillan, pp. 14–27.

Mulvey, Laura (1979), 'Feminism, Film and the *Avant-Garde*', in Mary Jacobus (ed.), *Women Writing and Writing About Women*, Beckenham: Croom Helm, pp. 177–95.

Murphy, Jeanette (1986), 'A Question of Silence', in Charlotte Brunsdon (ed.), *Films for Women*, London: BFI, pp. 99–108.

Nabokov, Vladimir ([1964] 1994), *The Luzhin Defense*, trans. Michael Scammell, Harmondsworth: Penguin.

Naremore James (2000), 'Introduction: Film and the Reign of Adaptation', in James Naremore (ed.), *Film Adaptation*, New Brunswick, New Jersey: Rutgers University Press, pp. 1–16.

Neale, Steve (1980), *Genre*, London: BFI.

Nealon, Christopher (2007), 'The Poetic Case', *Critical Inquiry* 33.4: 865–86.

Negra, Diane (2009), *What a Girl Wants? Fantasizing the Reclamation of Self in Postfeminism*, London and New York: Routledge.

Nikolopoulou, Asimina Ino (2011), 'Urbanism, Transgression and the Feminist Re-appropriation of the Gaze: Contesting Gender Roles in *A Question of Silence*', Gender, Sexuality, and Urban Spaces: Conference 2011, GCWS Working Papers Collection, pp. 2–13.

Osborne, Nicola (2001), Review of *The Luzhin Defence*, *Eye For Film* January 19. Last accessed 10 October 2024, at: https://www.eyeforfilm.co.uk/review/the-luzhin-defence-film-review-by-nicola-osborne.

Palmer, Augusta (1998), 'Seven Question (*sic*) with Marleen Gorris, Director of "Mrs. Dalloway"', *Indiewire* February 23. Last accessed 10 October 2024, at: https://www.indiewire.com/features/general/seven-question-with-marleen-gorris-director-of-mrs-dalloway-83082/.

Pidduck, Julianne (2004), *Contemporary Costume Film: Space, Place and the Past*, London: BFI.

Piercy, Marge (1983), 'A Story Wet as Tears', in Marge Piercy, *Stone, Paper, Knife*, London: Pandora, p. 15.

Poole, Steven (2000), 'The Nabokov Gambit', *The Guardian* August 25. Last accessed 10 October 2024, at: https://www.theguardian.com/books/2000/aug/25/classics.vladimirnabokov.

Radtke, H. Lorraine, and Henderikus J. Stam (eds.) (1995), *Power/Gender: Social Relations in Theory and Practice*, London: Sage.

Rakhimova-Sommers, Elena (2017), 'Introduction – Nabokov's Passportless Wanderer: A Study of Nabokov's Woman', in Elena Kakhimova-Sommers (ed.), *Nabokov's Women*, Lanham: Lexington Books, pp. xv–xxxi.

Ramanathan, Geetha (1992), 'Murder as Speech: Narrative Subjectivity in Marleen Gorris' *A Question of Silence*', *Genders* 15: 59–71.

Ramanathan, Geetha (2006), *Feminist Auteurs*, London and New York: Wallflower.

Ray Robert B. (2000), 'The Field of "Literature and Film"', in James Naremore (ed.), *Film Adaptation*, New Brunswick, New Jersey: Rutgers University Press, pp. 38–53.

Rees, Jasper (2011), 'Emily Watson: 'I'm a Character Actor – Who Gets Laid'. In *The Telegraph*, 26 March. Last accessed 10 October 2024, at: https://www.telegraph.co.uk/culture/film/starsandstories/8406563/Emily-Watson-Im-a-character-actor-who-gets-laid.html.

Reinhardt, Bernd (2011), 'Within the Whirlwind: Stalin's Great Terror and a Big Question Mark'. World Socialist Web Site, 13 June. Last accessed

10 October 2024, at: https://www.wsws.org/en/articles/2011/06/ whir-j13.html (Accessed 6 April 2021).

Rich, Adrienne (1979), 'When We Dead Awaken: Writing as Re-Vision', in Adrienne Rich, *On Lies, Secrets and Silence*, New York: W. W. Norton and Company, pp. 33–49.

Rich, B. Ruby ([1984] 1998), 'Lady Killers: A Question of Silence', in B. Ruby Rich, *Chick Flicks*, Durham, NC, and London: Duke University Press, pp. 319–25.

Rich, B. Ruby (1998), *Chick Flicks*, Durham and London: Duke University Press.Riley, Denise (1988), *Am I That Name?* Basingstoke: Palgrave Macmillan.

Riley, Denise ([2012] 2020), 'Time Lived, Without its Flow', in Denise Riley, *Say Something Back/ Time Lived, Without its Flow*, New York: New York Review Books, pp. 69–124.

Root, Jane (1986), 'Distributing *A Question of Silence* – A Cautionary Tale', in Charlotte Brunsdon (ed.), *Films for Women*, London: BFI, pp. 213–23.

Rose, Phyllis (1986), *Woman of Letters: A Life of Virginia* Woolf, London: Pandora.

Rosenbaum, Jonathan (2001), 'Defenseless', *Chicago Reader* May 3. Accessed at: https://chicagoreader.com/film/defenseless/.

Rousseau, Jean-Jacques ([1762] 1974), *Emile*, trans. Barbara Foxley, London: J. M. Dent.

Rowe, Kathleen (1995), *The Unruly Woman: Gender and the Genres of Laughter*, Austin: University of Texas Press.

Rowe Karlyn, Kathleen (2011), *Unruly Girls, Unrepentant Mothers*, Austin: University of Texas Press.

Rubin, Jeffrey A. (1996), 'Defining Resistance: Contested Interpretations of Everyday Acts', *Studies in Law, Politics, and Society* 15: 237–60.

Russo, Mary (1988), 'Female Grotesques: Carnival and Theory', in Teresa de Lauretis (ed.), *Feminist Studies/Critical Studies*, Houndmills, Basingstoke: Macmillan, pp. 213–29.

Russo, Mary (1999), 'Aging and the Scandal of Anachronism', in Kathleen Woodward (ed.), *Figuring Age*, Bloomington and Indianapolis: Indiana University Press, pp. 20–33.

Rybina, Polina (2018), 'Film Adaptation as the Art of Expansion: The Visual Poetics of Marleen Gorris' *Mrs. Dalloway*', *English Literature* 5, December: 59–75.

Sarris, Andrew (1998), 'A Bright, Wicked Mrs. Dalloway Disgraces a Salacious Dickens', *Observer* February 16. Last accessed 10 October 2024, at: https:// observer.com/1998/02/a-bright-wicked-mrs-dalloway-disgraces-a-sala-cious-dickens/.

Schmidt, Paul (2007), *The Stray Dog Cabaret: A Book of Russian Poems*, trans. Paul Schmidt, ed. Catherine Ciepiela and Honor Moore, New York: New York Review of Books.

Schwartzbaum, Lisa (1998), Review of *Mrs Dalloway, Entertainment Weekly* March 6. Last accessed 21 October 2024, at: https://web.archive.org/web/20190414221221/https://ew.com/article/1998/03/06/mrs-dalloway-2/amp/.

Scott, A. O. (2001), 'A Genius Pulled Apart by Both Love and Chess', *New York Times* April 20, p. E10.

Sellery, J'Nan Morse (2001), 'Women's Communities and the Magical Realist Gaze of *Antonia's Line*', *Philological Papers* 48: 115–24.

Seltzer, Mark (1998), *Serial Killers: Life and Death in America's Wound Culture*, New York and London: Routledge.

Sexton, Anne (2001/1971), 'The Frog Prince', in Anne Sexton, *Transformations*, Boston: Houghton Mifflin, pp. 93–100.

Showalter, Elaine (1981), 'Feminist Criticism in the Wilderness', *Critical Inquiry* 8.2: 179–205.

Showalter, Elaine (1992), 'Introduction' to Virginia Woolf's *Mrs. Dalloway*, London: Penguin, pp. xi–xlviii.

Shulman, Milton (1983), Review of *A Question of Silence, The Standard* 17 February, p. 23.

Simpson, Philip (2000), *Psycho Paths*, Carbondale and Edwardsville: Southern Illinois University Press.

Sinyard, Neil (1997), 'A Question of Gorris', *Dutch Crossing*, 21.2: 100–16.

Skarvellis, Jackie (1983), Review of *A Question of Silence, Morning Star* 18 February, p. 2.

Sklar, Robert (1996), 'The Lighter Side of Feminism: an Interview with Marlene Gorris', *Cineaste* 22.1: 26–8.

Smelik, Anneke (1990), 'Eilanddepressie (Island Depression)', *Het Nederlands Scenario* 3 ('Drie scenarios van Marleen Gorris'), Amsterdam: International Theatre and Film Books, pp. 247–55.

Smelik, Anneke (1993), 'And the Mirror Cracked: Metaphors of Violence in the Films of Marleen Gorris', *Women's Studies Int. Forum*, 16.4: 349–63.

Smelik, Anneke (1998), *And the Mirror Cracked: Feminist Cinema and Film Theory*, London: Palgrave Macmillan.

Smelik, Anneke (2023), 'Mirrors, Murders and Metaphors in the Films of Marleen Gorris', 20-page booklet for re-issuing of DVD-set. Cult Epics Distribution, USA.

Smith, Barbara Herrnstein (1981), 'Afterthoughts on Narrative: Narrative Versions, Narrative Theories', in W. J. T. Mitchell (ed) *On Narrative*, Chicago and London: University of Chicago Press, pp. 209–32.

Smith, Joan (1989), *Misogynies*, London: Faber and Faber.

Smith, Stacy L., Marc Choueiti, Angel Choi and Katherine Pieper (2019), 'Inclusion in the Director's Chair: Gender, Race and Age Across Directors Across 1,200 Top Films from 2007 to 2018', USC Annenberg, Inclusion

Initiative. Last accessed 10 October 2024, at http://assets.uscannenberg. org/docs/inclusion-in-the-directors-chair-2019.pdf.

Stevenson, Robert Louis ([1883] 2018), *Treasure Island*, Ware: Wordsworth Editions.

Stone, Alan A. (2001), 'No Defense', *Boston Review* June 1. Accessed at: https://www.bostonreview.net/articles/no-defense/.

Sweet, Matthew (1998), 'No Wonder it Knocked them for Six', *Independent on Sunday* March 8, Section 2, p. 6.

Thomas, Kevin (1996), '*Antonia's Line* Draws on Strength of Family, Women', *Los Angeles Times* 2 February. Last accessed 10 October 2024, at: https:// www.latimes.com/archives/la-xpm-1996-02-02-ca-31534-story.html.

Toker, Leona (2016), *Nabokov: The Mystery of Literary Structures*, Ithaca: Cornell University Press.

Tolczyk, Dariusz (2005), 'The Uses of Vulnerability: Literature and Ideology in Eugeniia Ginzburg's Memoir of the Gulag', *Literature & History* 14.1: 56–74.

Tulloch, John (1990), *Television Drama: Agency, Audience and Myth*, London: Routledge & Kegan Paul.

Verne, Jules ([1875] 2019), *The Mysterious Island*, trans. W. H. G. Kingston, Orinda, California: Seawolf Press.

Vidal, Bélen (2005), 'Playing in a Minor Key: The Literary Past through the Feminist Imagination', in Mireia Aragay (ed.), *Books in Motion*, Amsterdam: Rodopi, pp. 263–85.

Vidal, Bélen (2012), *Heritage Film: Nation, Genre and Representation*, London: Wallflower.

Volkmann, Laurenz (2011), 'Fortified Masculinity: Daniel Defoe's *Robinson Crusoe* as a Literary Emblem of Western Male Identity', in Stefan Horlacher (ed.), *Constructions of Masculinity in British Literature from the Middle Ages to the Present*, London: Palgrave Macmillan, pp. 129–46.

Walker, Nancy (1995), *The Disobedient Writer*, Austin: University of Texas Press.

Walters, Susanna Danuta (1991), '*Premature Postmortems*: "Postfeminism" and Popular Culture', *New Politics* Winter: 103–12.

Watts, Carol (1998), 'Time and the Working Mother: Kristeva's "Women's Time" Revisited', *Radical Philosophy* 91: 6–17.

Wigan, Michael (1982), Review of *A Question of Silence*, *The Scotsman* 21 August, p. 6.

Williams, Linda (1988), 'A Jury of their Peers: Marlene Gorris's *A Question of Silence*', in E. Ann Kaplan (ed.), *Postmodernism and its Discontents*, London: Verso, pp. 107–15.

Wilmington, Michael (1996), 'Independence Days', *Chicago Tribune* 14 February: https://www.chicagotribune.com/news/ct-xpm-1996-02-14-9602140183-story.html (last accessed 21 September 2023).

Wilmington, Michael (1998), 'Vanessa Redgrave Shines in 'Mrs. Dalloway', *Chicago Tribune* March 6: https://www.chicagotribune.com/news/ct-xpm-1998–03–06–9803060283-story.html (last accessed 27 November 2023).

Woolf, Virginia ([1925] 1992), *Mrs Dalloway*, Harmondsworth: Penguin.

Woolf, Virginia ([1929] 1993), 'A Room of One's Own', in Michèle Barrett (ed.), *A Room of One's Own and Three Guineas*, Harmondsworth: Penguin, pp. 1–114.

Woolf, Virginia ([1938] 1993), 'Three Guineas', in Michèle Barrett (ed.), *A Room of One's Own and Three Guineas*, Harmondsworth: Penguin, pp. 115–334.

Wreyford, Natalie and Shelley Cobb (2017), 'Data and Responsibility: Toward a Feminist Methodology for Producing Historical Data on Women in the Contemporary Film Industry', *Feminist Media Histories* 3.3: 107–32.

Wyss, Johann Rudolf ([1812] 2012), *The Swiss Family Robinson*, London: William Collins.

Films

A Question of Silence (De Stilte Rond Christine M) (1982), directed by Marleen Gorris. Netherlands: Quartet Films.

A Room with a View (1986), directed by James Ivory. UK: Merchant Ivory Productions.

Antonia's Line (Antonia) (1995), directed by Marleen Gorris. Netherlands: Eurimages.

Bridget Jones's Diary (2001), directed by Sharon Maguire. USA/UK/France: Universal Pictures.

Brief Encounter (1945), directed by David Lean. UK: Eagle-Lion.

Broken Mirrors (Gebroken Spiegels) (1984), directed by Marleen Gorris. Netherlands: Sigma Film Productions.

Carolina (2003), directed by Marleen Gorris. USA and Germany: Miramax.

Cast Away (2000), directed by Robert Zemeckis. USA: 20th Century Fox.

Clueless (1995), directed by Amy Heckerling. USA: Paramount Pictures.

Death Wish II (1982), directed by Michael Winner. USA: Columbia Pictures.

Dressed to Kill (1980), directed by Brian de Palma. USA: American International Pictures.

Eyes of a Stranger (1980), directed by Ken Wiederhorn. USA: Warner Bros.

The Eyes of Laura Mars (1978), directed by Irvin Kershner. USA: Columbia Pictures.

First Blood (1982), directed by Ted Kotcheff. USA: Orion Pictures.

He Knows You're Alone (1980), directed by Armand Mastroianni. USA: Metro-Goldwyn-Mayer.

Howards End (1992), directed by James Ivory. UK/US/Japan: Merchant Ivory Productions.

I Am Legend (2007), directed by Francis Lawrence. USA: Warner Bros.

The Last Island (1990), directed by Marleen Gorris. Netherlands: First Floor Features.

Lord of the Flies (1963), directed by Peter Brook. UK: British Lion Film Corporation.

Lord of the Flies (1990), directed by Harry Hook. USA: Columbia Pictures, Metro-Goldwyn-Mayer.

The Luzhin Defence (2000), directed by Marleen Gorris. UK/France: France 2 Cinema.

Mansfield Park (1999), directed by Patricia Rozema. UK: Buena Vista International.

Maurice (1987), directed by James Ivory. UK: Merchant Ivory Productions.

Mrs Dalloway (1997), directed by Marleen Gorris. UK/USA/Netherlands: First Look Pictures.

New York Ripper (1982), directed by Lucio Fulci. Italy: Fulvia Film.

Peeping Tom (1960), directed by Michael Powell.

The Portrait of a Lady (1996), directed by Jane Campion. UK/USA: Polygram.

The Prince and Me (2004), directed by Martha Coolidge. USA: Paramount Pictures.

Rocky III (1982), directed by Sylvester Stallone. USA: United Artists.

Sleepless in Seattle (1993), directed by Nora Ephron. USA: Tristar Pictures.

Sudden Impact (1983), directed by Clint Eastwood. USA: Warner Bros.

Swann in Love (1984), directed by Volker Schlöndorff. France, Germany: Orion Classics.

Sweet Home Alabama (2002), directed by Andy Tennant. USA: Buena Vista Pictures.

Washington Square (1997), directed by Agnieszka Holland. USA: Buena Vista Pictures.

When Harry Met Sally (1989), directed by Rob Reiner. USA: Columbia Pictures.

You've Got Mail (1998), directed by Nora Ephron. USA: Warner Bros.

Index

EU representative:
Easy Access System Europe
Mustamäe tee 50, 10621 Tallinn, Estonia
Gpsr.requests@easproject.com

www.ingramcontent.com/pod-product-compliance
Lightning Source LLC
Chambersburg PA
CBHW070757100426
42742CB00012B/2167